THE TIMELINE OF NATIVE AMERICANS

THE TIMELINE OF NATIVE AMERICANS

THE ULTIMATE GUIDE TO NORTH AMERICA'S INDIGENOUS PEOPLES

Greg O'Brien

THUNDER BAY
P·R·E·S·S

San Diego, California

Thunder Bay Press
An imprint of the Advantage Publishers Group
10350 Barnes Canyon Road, San Diego, CA 92121
www.thunderbaybooks.com

All notations of errors or omissions should be addressed to Thunder Bay Press,
Editorial Department, at the above address. All other correspondence (author inquiries,
permissions) concerning the content of this book should be addressed to
Amber Books Ltd., Bradley's Close, 74–77 White Lion Street, London N1 9PF,
United Kingdom. www.amberbooks.co.uk.

ISBN-13: 978-1-59223-861-3
ISBN-10: 1-59223-861-0

Project Editor: Sarah Uttridge
Picture Research: Natascha Spargo
Design: Jerry Williams

Printed in China

1 2 3 4 5 12 11 10 09 08

Contents

America Before 1492

The history of the Americas and American Indian history did not begin with the arrival of Christopher Columbus in the Caribbean in 1492. The ancestors of the people encountered by Columbus and later European explorers had lived in the Americas for up to 30,000 years.

Countless generations of American Indian peoples settled the land, built communities, raised families, and discovered new ways to utilize the environment and improve their standards of living. The "New World" was as much an "Old World" made up of diverse peoples with different languages and cultures, much like Europe or Asia. Some anthropologists adhere to the term "prehistory" to describe

Left: View of a kiva at Pueblo Bonito Ruins, Chaco Culture National Historic Park, New Mexico. Pueblo Bonito was a huge house built by the Anasazis c. 850. Right: A Navajo man wearing a woolen blanket and warming his hands over an open fire, c. 1915.

Indian peoples before European contact, but there is history wherever and whenever humans have lived, and the history of the Americas goes back tens of thousands of years. More accurate, therefore, is the term "precontact" to describe the deep history of the Americas before the arrival of Europeans, and then Africans, Asians, and others. The postcontact era after 1492 initiated unimaginable and enduring changes among the people, plants, animals, and environment of the Americas, and it is for that reason, as the format of this book demonstrates, that far more ink has been spilled on the period after 1492 than on the thousands of years before it.

Another reason for the uneven coverage of American Indian history has to do with sources. The origin of the term "prehistory" denotes peoples who left no written records, but even that definition is imperfect with reference to the Americas. Some Native peoples, such as the Aztecs and Mayas, left rich written records of their society's past, and, of course, all peoples, whether literate or not, inscribed iconography on structures, pottery, weapons, tools, and other items, telling stories about past events, people, or religious ideas. Many of these and other stories still exist today, having been passed down by American Indians through oral traditions and preserved rituals. European and Indian written documents postcontact provide us with insight into the deeper past, as well as chronicling events after Europeans arrived. As with

A statuette of the Aztec goddess Chalchiuhtlicue, goddess of water.

similar ancient civilizations the world over, however, much of what we know about peoples in the Americas thousands of years ago comes from archaeology. Like all sources of history, archaeology gives us an incomplete picture because of its reliance on material remains that have survived in some form to the present day. The thoughts and concerns of real people can be difficult to glean from these material remains, but archaeologists, like historians, have continued to refine their methods and

interpretations to arrive at an ever more detailed and better understanding of the past.

Population

One point of contention among scholars, Indian people, and the general public is over how many Indians lived in the Americas when Europeans first arrived. Although we will never know exactly what the population was at any given time, best estimates place the population for North America, excluding Mexico, at between 8 million and 12 million, with some estimates going as high as 18 million people. Mexico and Central America may have supported a population of up to 20 million, with many millions more living in South America and the Caribbean. Somewhere in the order of 43 million to 65 million people lived in all of the Americas before European contact, or about one-fifth of the world's total human population at that time.

Although the range of estimates allows for much variation, there is little doubt that millions of people lived in North America when Europeans began their conquest of the continent. The numbers matter, inasmuch as they have been revised upward in recent decades from a figure of

c. 75,000–45,000 BC

The first exposure of the Bering Land Bridge makes human migration from Asia to North America possible.

a million people or less living in North America, the figure promoted at the beginning of the twentieth century. No longer can America be accurately portrayed as a vast wilderness waiting to be filled up by determined European settlers, or as a land inhabited by only a few "nomadic savages" who lacked the foresight and abilities to build lasting communities. Such ideas gained wide acceptance from the time that Europeans first arrived in the Americas up to the nineteenth century, along with the ideology of "manifest destiny," the justification for dispossessing Native peoples of their lands. The displacement of millions of people by another population requires explanation and can no longer be hidden behind European and American fictions of empty continents and uncivilized peoples.

Origins

The question of where Native American ancestors came from, and when, is equally controversial. There is confirmed evidence of a settlement at Monte Verde in southern Chile dating to just over 12,000 years ago. Numerous other archaeological sites suggest pushing the date of the earliest settlements back as far as

Ruins in the Incan sacred valley of Ollantaytambo, near the famed Incan city of Machu Picchu, Peru.

c. 28,000–10,000 BC

Successive migrations of people occur, from northeast Asia to the Americas via the Bering Land Bridge, and by dugout canoes and skin boats along the western North American coast.

c. 14,000–10,000 BC

Humans enter the Great Plains in the heart of North America.

Mandan Indians of the upper Missouri River perform a bison-dance in front of their medicine lodge, c. 1840.

40,000 years ago. Intertwined with trying to understand the length of time that Indian people have lived in the Americas are theories about how they got there. The standard scientific theory suggests that peoples from northeast Asia migrated by foot over the Bering Land Bridge that became exposed at various times during the Ice Age from c. 75,000 BC to c. 8000 BC. The general consensus by those who support this theory is that the bulk of the migration occurred 12,000 to 14,000 years ago. Following large game herds, so the theory argues, these people migrated south and east over generations to eventually inhabit all of the Americas. However, the Monte Verde site in Chile suggests that people arrived in the far northwestern reaches of North America well in advance of 12,000 years ago—long enough to have established a permanent settlement at the southern end of South America. An alternative theory supported by recent archaeological work suggests that people traveled by small boats down the Pacific coast of the Americas, stopping off at various points to travel inland in Central and South America.

c. 11,000 BC

Clovis culture develops. Clovis Indians hunt large mammals and share technological and other information with their neighbors, resulting in the spread of Clovis spearheads throughout North America.

Whether or not a land or a sea migration makes more sense—and both types of migrations could have occurred simultaneously—many American Indian groups uphold that their origins are within the Americas. History in the Americas began for the Iroquois when their ancestors fell from the sky; for the Pueblos, Mandans, Navajos, and Choctaws it began when their ancestors emerged from under the ground; for the Kiowas it began when their ancestors emerged from a hollow log. Native traditions about where they came from and how they came into being almost invariably place them in the Americas rather than in some distant continent. Supporters of the Bering Land Bridge theory suggest that such oral traditions are quaint legends or that the migrations occurred so long ago as to be forgotten by contemporary Indians. However, Native people are sincere about being native to the Americas. The Miami chief Little Turtle famously told Thomas Jefferson that if American Indians appeared to be physically related to Asian people

Thomas Jefferson, third president of the United States and pioneering ethnologist of American Indian cultures.

it was because Asians had migrated from the Americas to Asia rather than the reverse. It is also possible that all of these theories may have elements of truth; Native people know they have always existed and that their ancestors have been in the Americas for countless generations.

Whether Indians have occupied the Americas for 12,000 years or longer, and that they originated in the Americas, are arguments with profound implications. Both Canada and the United States like to describe themselves as a "nation of immigrants" to highlight the experiences and histories that all Canadians and Americans have in common, and to emphasize that no one group has any more inherent claim to the territory of North America than another. This denies Indians their unique status in American history and the longevity of that history, and it glosses over the realities of how American Indians have been treated by European colonial powers and the succeeding American and Canadian governments.

Earliest Americans

Partly because archaeological evidence is scarcer the farther back in time we look for indications

---

c. 10,500 BC

The oldest confirmed village settlement is founded in the Americas at Monte Verde, Chile.

c. 10,000–7000 BC

The final Ice Age. Glaciers recede, the Bering Land Bridge disappears underwater, and the climate of the Americas changes dramatically, becoming warmer and more varied.

American Indians of the Paleo-Indian era hunted woolly mammoths and other animals for meat, clothing, and tools.

of human habitation in North America, the earliest phase of American Indian history—the so-called Paleo-Indian (ancient Indian) period, c. 13,000 BC to c. 8000 BC—is described by archaeologists in only general terms. The primary archaeological evidence for these early Paleo-Indians is long, fluted, chipped stone spearheads. These early points are named "Clovis" after the Clovis, New Mexico, archaeological site where the point type was first recognized. By around 10,000 BC, the Paleo-Indians appear to have occupied most of the North American continent. Since the main evidence for these ancient peoples are their durable stone spearheads, archaeologists have long described Paleo-Indians as big-game hunters. Paleo-Indians hunted large mammals such as mammoths, and they may have played a part in the extinction of mammoths and other megafauna of the Late Pleistocene. However, climate change is more likely to have played the determinative role in these extinctions. What the Paleo-Indian archaeological evidence does not tell us with much certainty is how these people lived. It is unknown whether mammoth hunting was a constant pursuit or a once-in-a-lifetime

c. 9000 BC

Plant cultivation and agriculture emerge in Mexico. Indian people nurture wild grasses that will eventually evolve into varieties of corn.

event. Information about political organizations, religious views, and gender roles are similarly unknown for this era. According to archaeologists, Paleo-Indian campsites were places where bands of up to a few dozen people stopped for a few

Flint projectile points found in New Mexico are typical of hunting and tool technology of the precontact era.

weeks or months. They spent their year moving after game animals, visiting flint quarries to make spearheads, and joining other groups, probably in the summer, to trade and interact. In the winter, when game became scarce and hunting was most difficult, the bands broke up into smaller family units in order to survive. Nevertheless, the uniformity of Clovis spearheads throughout North America may provide a false picture of cultural similarity.

It is more likely that, as soon as people arrived in the Americas, regional cultural variety developed around different climates and the availability of different resources. Toward the end of the Pleistocene period around 10,000 years ago, North America began to warm, and the flora and fauna in any given environment became more diverse. Before the industrial age and modern transportation systems, all peoples in North America were dependent on the natural resources available for food, clothing, and

A Hupa Indian man of California fishes for salmon with a spear, a traditional method of hunting for game.

c. 8800 BC

Cooperation between bands is apparent from the Lindenmeier site in northern Colorado.

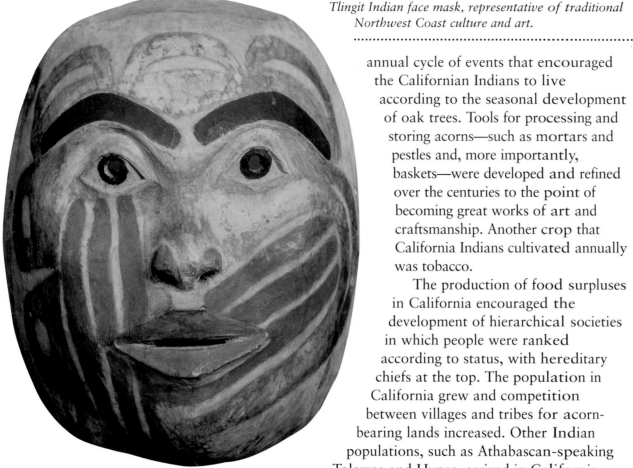

Tlingit Indian face mask, representative of traditional Northwest Coast culture and art.

annual cycle of events that encouraged the Californian Indians to live according to the seasonal development of oak trees. Tools for processing and storing acorns—such as mortars and pestles and, more importantly, baskets—were developed and refined over the centuries to the point of becoming great works of art and craftsmanship. Another crop that California Indians cultivated annually was tobacco.

The production of food surpluses in California encouraged the development of hierarchical societies in which people were ranked according to status, with hereditary chiefs at the top. The population in California grew and competition between villages and tribes for acorn-bearing lands increased. Other Indian populations, such as Athabascan-speaking Tolowas and Hupas, arrived in California between the tenth and thirteenth centuries to share in California's bounty. Extensive regional trade networks spread foodstuffs and technology throughout California and the surrounding areas. California became one of the most densely populated areas in North America before European contact, with many villages numbering over a thousand people, and a total population of over 300,000 by the 1490s.

The Great Basin

In the Great Basin between the Rocky Mountains to the east and the Sierra Nevada to the west, there exists tremendous environmental and topographical diversity. In general, however, the area has been characterized by arid conditions since at least 4000 BC, which make agricultural growth difficult, if not impossible. The Indian peoples who lived in this region were forced to develop intricate strategies to find food and water throughout the year. They moved within the Great Basin according to the time of year and subsisted from hunting and gathering. Some Great Basin peoples who lived along the shores of Pyramid Lake and the Walker River in Nevada lived in sedentary

c. 4500–2500 BC

Modern species of bison evolve on the Great Plains.

c. 3500 BC

The first mounds in North America are constructed in the lower Mississippi valley.

villages and harvested fish year-round, supplementing their diet through hunting and gathering. Seed harvesting and processing became a major pursuit for Great Basin Indian women, and evidence of seed-processing tools date from at least 10,000 years ago. Material culture for most Great Basin peoples consisted of animal-hide clothing, together with tools made from various animal parts, wood, and stone.

From around 400, horticultural communities growing corn and living in semipermanent pit

Pyramid Lake, Nevada, where some Great Basin peoples lived in permanent settlements and relied primarily on fishing for sustenance.

Reconstruction of a Yurok sweat lodge in California, typical of Native architecture created for sacred rituals.

c. 3000 BC

Aleut and Inuit peoples arrive in Alaska.

Pottery first emerges in the Southeast.

houses emerged in Utah, eastern Nevada, western Colorado, and southern Idaho. Called "Fremont culture" by archaeologists, this horticultural phase had disappeared by about 1300, as drought struck many areas of North America. The former horticultural peoples moved out of the region or radically altered their lifestyles. They were replaced by the Numic-speaking forebears of the Utes and Shoshones, who had slowly migrated east from California and relied on hunting and gathering. The Shoshones subsequently moved further east, out of the Great Basin and into the western plains, where they established an annual trade gathering that attracted peoples from the plains, the Great Basin, and Columbia River regions. The example of the Shoshones is suggestive of how much migration and change had occurred among American Indians well before Europeans arrived in the fifteenth and sixteenth centuries. The Indian groups who continued to hunt and gather in the Great Basin adapted to the harsh climate by knowing precisely which plants and

A Shoshone man, c. 1899. Over decades, the Shoshones migrated from California to the Great Plains.

animals were available during the year. Their knowledge of the land and the environment became intimately wrapped up in their religious beliefs and ceremonial cycle, and their survival depended on strict adherence to rules of proper interaction between humankind and nature.

The Plains

Stereotypically, when we think of Plains Indians, or Indians in general, we imagine people on horseback, wearing flowing war bonnets and hunting buffalo, but that reality never existed on the plains until after Europeans had arrived in North America. Horses were introduced by Europeans, and Plains Indians did not develop a horse-based buffalo-hunting culture until the eighteenth and nineteenth centuries.

One element of the stereotype known to be true is that Plains Indians did hunt buffalo before European contact. Ever since Paleo-Indian times, Plains Indians hunted bison on foot. They may have had some help from domesticated dogs, which they used to help transport their belongings as they traveled over the plains. In addition to using Clovis spearheads to kill bison, groups of hunters also employed buffalo drives

c. 2500 BC

The earliest corn is grown in the southwestern and southeastern regions of North America.

and corrals to drive groups of bison into small areas or over cliffs. These communal hunting techniques required greater degrees of social organization and cooperation than previous methods of hunting single animals. Indians stationed themselves along a preplanned route, making noises and waving their arms, while runners, perhaps using fire, guided buffalo herds toward the cliffs. As the buffalo panicked, they followed one another over the precipice to certain death. The oldest, largest, and best-preserved buffalo drive site is the Head-Smashed-In buffalo jump in Alberta, Canada. For more than 7,000 years, Plains Indians drove buffalo over the cliffs at this site. Dozens of animals might be killed or injured at once, requiring hundreds of men and women to process the carcasses for meat, fur, and other body parts. Plains Indians used as much of the bison as possible: the muscle and fat provided food, the hides were used to make shelter and clothing, and the bones and organs were used to make utensils. Some buffalo resources were undoubtedly wasted at the jump sites because more animals died than people were able to handle. Another major innovation in hunting and warfare—the bow and arrow   had spread to the plains from the north by about 1000 and further contributed to reliance on hunting bison.

Hunting bison remained a vital part of Plains Indian existence during the nineteenth century,

Buffalo provided the primary source of meat, clothing, and tools for Plains Indians for thousands of years.

c. 2000 BC

Inuit people move east across northern Canada, spreading out all the way to Greenland. Inuit cultures develop unique technology and lifestyles to adapt to the harsh extremes of the far northern climate.

but many Plains Indian groups developed horticulture beginning around 400. First appearing in the northeastern plains among peoples connected with villages and agriculture east of the Mississippi River, corn and other crops spread among the river valleys of the plains. By 1500 the Siouan-speaking Mandans and Hidatsas, and the Caddoan-speaking Arikaras, inhabited the Missouri River valley and built villages along ridgetops overlooking the river. Their towns became major centers of trade as buffalo hunters exchanged robes and meat for crops, baskets, and other products. Pawnees established a presence on the Platte River system and relied on a mixed agricultural and buffalo-hunting culture that melded with their belief system so that corn harvests and buffalo hunts depended on each other for success.

In the centuries before European contact, the plains were a dynamic place characterized by migrating buffalo herds, agriculture along the rivers, and the movement of peoples in and out.

....

Typical topography of the Southwest, where Athabascan-speaking peoples lived after migrating.

c. 1500 BC

Native people at the Bat Cave, New Mexico, acquire cultivated corn seeds from Mexico.

Other Siouan-speaking peoples, such as the Kansas, Otos, Missouris, Poncas, and Omahas, migrated into the plains from the East and tended to combine agriculture with buffalo hunting. Athabascan-speakers migrated south from western Canada from the eighth century. A massive volcano eruption near the White River in Alaska in 720 may have spurred the migration of Athabascans away from that area. Their descendants among the Navajos and Apaches in the Southwest, the Tolowas and Hupas of northern California, and various groups in the Mackenzie valley of northwestern Canada, retain traditions of that event. The Athabascans came into contact on the southern plains with the Wichitas and Jumanos, and became important trade middlemen between the Pueblo Indians of the Southwest and Plains Indian groups. As the Athabascans continued to move south during the centuries before European contact, the areas they vacated became inhabited by the Blackfeet, the Crows, the Cheyennes, and the Arapahos. This configuration of peoples on the plains was still changing when Europeans arrived, and it altered again because of European intrusion and the introduction of diseases, guns, and horses.

Indians of the Atlantic coast of Virginia and the Carolinas, as depicted by Theodore de Bry, c. 1585, showing bow-and-arrow technology and hunting techniques.

c. 1000 BC

Southwestern people acquire squash and bean seeds from Mexico.

The Poverty Point mound site is constructed in Louisiana.

The Southwest

The Southwest stands out as the first location in North America where people practiced agriculture on a significant scale. Around 3,500 years ago, women in New Mexico acquired new seeds from their neighbors to the south. The seeds were corn, which had been cultivated by Indian peoples in central Mexico since 5000 BC. Over the centuries, southwestern peoples began to rely more heavily on corn as a primary part of the diet, and then, 3,000 years ago, they gained seeds of bean and gourd plants from their southern neighbors. Corn does not grow without human care and cultivation. Indian people (primarily women) selected and developed corn and other plant varieties that grew best in their particular environment. Once the triad of corn, beans, and squash came together, southwestern Indians began producing surpluses of food that enabled them to establish permanently located villages. Corn, beans, and squash became the "three sisters" of North American diets and revolutionized Indian lifestyles throughout the continent. The three crops grow well together and were therefore planted simultaneously in small mounds, with corn at the top. Bean plants restored the nitrogen that was leached from the soil by the corn, the nitrogen fertilized the corn, and the bean vines grew up the corn stalk. Gourd vines and their leaves spread over the ground at the bases of the corn plants, suppressing weeds. The plants also work well when eaten together because beans greatly increase the nutritional value of corn by releasing lysine, an amino acid crucial to human health.

In the highlands of the New Mexico–Arizona border area, Mogollon people grew corn and squash. They initially lived in pit houses built partially underground, but later constructed multiunit apartment buildings aboveground. In order to transport and store food, the Mogollons used baskets and began making clay pots around 200 in the distinctive black-on-white Mimbres style. Pottery was

A Hopi woman preparing food in a traditional manner typical of agriculturally minded peoples from the Southwest, c. 1922.

c. 800–100 BC

Adena culture dominates in the eastern woodlands. Adena people construct conical earthen mounds and circular earthworks, including the Great Serpent Mound in Ohio.

widespread throughout the Southwest by 500. However, the Mogollon culture declined around 1100 and became absorbed by the Anasazi culture.

Agriculture requires water, which meant that Indians living in the arid Southwest either lived near water sources, such as rivers, or developed ways to transport water to the fields. By AD 500, the Hohokam culture that developed in southwestern Arizona and then spread outward had constructed miles of irrigation canals, some as long as ten miles, to guide rain and river water to the villages. They were then able to produce two crops of corn, beans, and squash per year in an area that experienced little annual rainfall. The Hohokams were the ancestors of the Akimel O'odham (Pimas) and the Tohono O'odham (Papagos). The Hohokam network of canals eventually transported water hundreds of miles and removed Hohokam dependence on the local Gila River. The Hohokams traded heavily with central Mexico, and Mexican influences are apparent in

their architecture and material remains. The Hohokams also engaged in trade that brought them items from the plains and California. Snaketown—their largest village, located near

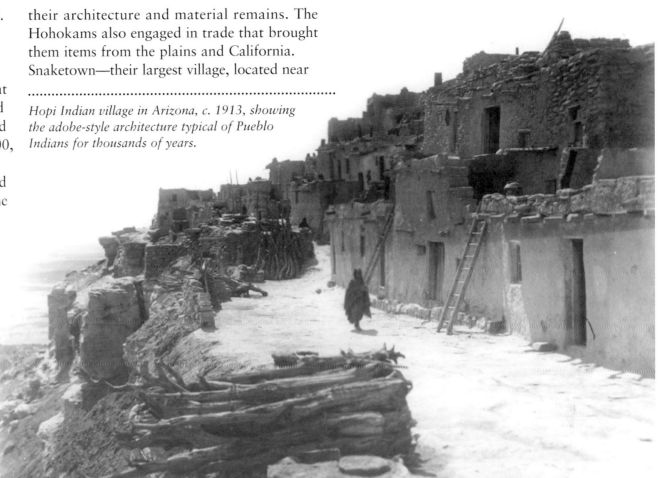

Hopi Indian village in Arizona, c. 1913, showing the adobe-style architecture typical of Pueblo Indians for thousands of years.

c. 100 BC–AD 500

Hopewell people decorate pottery and participate in trade networks that bring exotic materials (copper, mica, obsidian, and shell) to the eastern woodlands.

Hopewell culture flourishes in the eastern woodlands. They depend on hunting, fishing, agriculture, and collecting wild plant food. Hopewell people construct earthen burial mounds and complex earthworks.

what is now Phoenix, Arizona—supported a population of nearly 600 for over 1,200 years. However, Hohokam culture declined around 1300 after either prolonged drought or increased water salinity.

With agricultural knowledge, likely gained from the Hohokams, a new culture known as Anasazis (Navajo for "ancient ones") developed in the Four Corners region where New Mexico, Arizona, Utah, and Colorado meet. Building on the farming success and architectural styles of the Mogollons, the Anasazis emerged around 900 and reached their height of power between 1100 and 1300. Anasazi people grew and stored corn and other crops, wove and decorated baskets, made pottery, became students of astronomy, and designed complex buildings and cities. They supplemented their diets through hunting, used the bow and arrow, domesticated turkeys for food and ceremonial purposes, and grew and wove cotton into clothing and blankets. In some cases they built large sites, such as Chaco Canyon in northwestern New Mexico, which

Indians of the Southwest carved petroglyphs to mark trails, sacred sites, and historic events.

c. 100–1400

Hohokam culture is preeminent in the Southwest. The Hohokam people cultivate corn, beans, and squash, and also grow cotton, agave, and other native plants. They supplement this diet by hunting and gathering local plants.

Many Indian groups, especially in the Southwest, kept domesticated turkeys.

....

included Pueblo Bonito, a building that had hundreds of rooms and may have housed many people. The Chaco Canyon complex of numerous buildings and satellite communities supported a total population of around 15,000. It was also the focal point of an immense regional trade network with more than 400 miles of straight roads and walkways carved through rock connecting one site to another. Other Anasazi sites are located throughout the Four Corners region. Some, such as Mesa Verde in southwestern Colorado, are made up of dozens of multistoried buildings carved into the sides of mountains, accessible only by ladder from below or by rope from above.

Anasazi culture declined in the thirteenth century when a series of droughts struck the region and warfare increased. Without food surpluses, and under increasing threat, the Anasazis moved south into the Rio Grande valley and eventually became some of the Pueblo Indians who greeted the Spanish in the mid-sixteenth century. The dispersal of the Anasazis took on a religious dimension as they spread throughout the Southwest their use of kivas (circular underground chambers where rituals and meetings occurred). They also adopted as their own the kachina spirits of other Pueblo peoples. Kachinas are responsible for bringing rain and bountiful harvest, among other duties, which may explain Anasazi willingness to adopt the new ideas as they moved south and east.

....

Southwestern Indians—such as the Anasazis and later Pueblo groups—used circular kivas for ceremonies.

c. 500

At Snaketown and other sites in the Gila River valley in Arizona, Indian people build irrigation canals.

The emergence of new Pueblo and O'odham peoples in the Southwest coincided with the arrival of Déné (Athabascan) speakers from the north beginning around 1300. These new arrivals, whom we currently know better as Navajos and Apaches, tended to settle in areas that the Anasazis had abandoned. Initially, the newcomers relied primarily on hunting for food, but they soon developed a lucrative trade with the more established Pueblo peoples, exchanging meat and furs for crops, baskets, ceramics, and cloth. The eastern Apaches, in particular, who lived on the southwestern plains east of the Pueblos, brought new trade items from the East into the Southwest, greatly expanding the range and importance of regional trade networks. The Navajos settled in northern Arizona and adopted many of the farming practices of their Pueblo neighbors. The strong relationship between the Athabascan speakers and the Pueblos played an important role in shaping the southwestern Indian response to the Spanish arrival.

A family of Apaches, c. 1909, using traditional housing, and a mixture of traditional and manufactured clothing.

c. 500–1200

The bow and arrow first appears and is quickly adapted for use in war and hunting.

Population increases, especially in the eastern woodlands, and large villages develop. Indians continue to grow crops of squash, goosefoot, and maygrass, and some communities begin to grow corn around 800.

Eastern Woodlands

East of the Mississippi River, Native peoples became distinguished for their agriculture, trade, complex town and mound constructions, and strict social hierarchy. Eastern Indians began domesticating indigenous seed plants such as sunflowers, squash, and marsh elder as much as 4,000 years ago. Corn spread into the East after it became a staple in the Southwest, arriving in Tennessee by 350 BC, in the Ohio valley by 300 BC, and in the Illinois valley by AD 650. Along with domesticated crops came pottery and baskets to transport, store, and cook them. Eastern Indians carved soft stones, such as steatite and sandstone, and they fashioned gourd bottles for food storage. Highly valued items, such as copper from the Great Lakes and wampum shells from the northeastern coast, were acquired by trade throughout the East. Agricultural surpluses and abundant wild food enabled eastern Indians to develop large towns, and to encourage religious, artistic, and political specialization.

....

Miamisburg Mound in Ohio, built by the Adena people between 800 BC and AD 100.

Over a period of nearly 4,000 years, eastern Indians constructed tens of thousands of earthen mounds. The oldest site, which consists of eleven mounds, dates to over 5,000 years ago and is located near Watson Brake, Louisiana; it predates all other mound sites in the Americas by nearly 2,000 years. At Poverty Point in Louisiana, approximately 2,500 people lived near or regularly visited a mound site composed of concentric rings and other earthworks dating to about 3,000 years ago. The site included several mounds, the largest of which was 640 feet by 710 feet and in the shape of a falcon. Poverty Point was a regional trade center that received goods from throughout eastern and central North America.

c. 600

The Spiro site is founded on the Red River in Oklahoma.

Mounds located at Mound City Group National Monument in Ohio are representative of the accomplishments and religious expression of the Hopewell culture.

c. 700

The Cahokia metropolis is
established along the Mississippi
River in southern Illinois.

The Etowah chiefdom is
established in Georgia.

700–1600

Mississippian societies flourish in the Southeast, creating a culture characterized by
mound building, hierarchical social structure, corn growing, long-distance trade, and
highly developed artistic and spiritual expression.

Its localized power extended outward when labor from surrounding communities, either coerced or voluntary, was used to build the various structures. Social ranking also existed at Poverty Point, as shown through certain rare, elite items found only in burials at one location near the largest mound. By 700 BC, Poverty Point had lost its dominant position and elite status, although the reasons for this remain unclear.

By 100 BC, the Adena culture emerged in the Ohio valley. Adena peoples constructed hundreds of large mound centers and burial mounds that commemorated the dead. Adena culture also engaged in a far-flung trade network that brought mica from North Carolina and copper from the Great Lakes into the Ohio valley. They constructed immense effigy mounds representing various animals. The most famous of these is the Great Serpent Mound in southern Ohio, which stretches more than 1,300 feet in length along a ridgetop and has an average height of 3 feet 3 inches. The serpent's head appears to be swallowing an egg or some other elliptical shape, but the precise meaning of the effigy is unknown. Adena burial mounds rest nearby, which have led

archaeologists to believe that the serpent was built by Adena peoples. However, recent scholarship suggests either an earlier construction before the Adenas or a later construction by the Hopewells or other peoples.

Adena culture merged around AD 100 with the Hopewell culture, which had originated further west in the Illinois valley. Hopewellian people built more elaborate burial mounds and earthen architecture, and developed greater ceremonial complexity, with ceremonial centers spread over many acres and composed of dozens of mounds. Hopewell exchange networks brought in trade items from all over North America: copper from the Great Lakes; mica, chlorite, and quartz from the southern Appalachians; obsidian from the Yellowstone region in Montana; conch and turtle shells, shark and alligator teeth, and barracuda jaws from Florida; galena (lead sulfide ore ground to a

powder to make white paint) from the Mississippi valley; flint from Indiana; quartz from North Dakota; and silver from the upper regions of the Great Lakes. Hopewell artisans made engraved works and other objects for elite patrons. Elites appear to have controlled the trade networks and the religious expression of Hopewell culture. By around 400, the Hopewell tradition declined in power and influence. The reasons

....

A necklace of animal teeth and bones that may have been used in trade among eastern Indians.

900

The Plains Indian tradition of sedentary farming villages appears along rivers and streams, and includes the introduction of corn and beans.

The Ocmulgee site is established in Georgia.

era (about 1000 to 1700). Centered in the middle and lower Mississippi River valley and throughout the Southeast, Mississippian culture was characterized by cleared-field agriculture, mound construction, matrilineal kinship, social hierarchy, and a chiefdom political structure. Although Mississippian communities ranged in size from simple chiefdoms of one village to paramount chiefdoms with cities and satellite communities, they shared general cultural traits.

The foremost Mississippian site is Cahokia, just east of present-day St. Louis, where the Missouri and Mississippi rivers meet to form a vast, nutrient-rich floodplain. According to archaeologists, the city of Cahokia was inhabited from about 700 to 1400. At its peak, from 1050 to 1200, the city covered nearly six square miles, and possibly as many as 20,000 people lived there. More than 120 mounds were built over time, and most mounds were enlarged several times. North America's largest earthen structure before European contact was the platform mound at Cahokia known as Monks

Algonquian Indian men preparing for the gender-defined activities of war, hunting, and sports, c. 1591.

c. 1000

Beans are first cultivated in the Southeast.

Plains village traditions emerge on the central plains.

Mound. This comprised at least 22 million cubic feet of dirt, all carried by humans using large baskets, and built over the course of two centuries. Some of the mounds supported wooden structures thought to be homes or temples for political elites and religious specialists. Circles of wooden posts may have served as solar calendars, while wooden palisades surrounded the core of the city to protect against attack. Ball games and ceremonies took place in the immense plaza in front of Monks Mound. Burials at Cahokia show dramatic status differentiation, with some elites being buried with pierced shell disks, sheets of copper and mica, hundreds of arrowheads, and hundreds of human sacrifices. Houses clustered around mounds probably represented particular kinship lineages, while the main agricultural fields lay outside the city center. Numerous satellite communities surrounding Cahokia grew corn and hunted deer and other animals to help feed people in the metropolis. Cahokia became a major trade center, where raw materials and finished products from all over eastern and central North America were exchanged. By the

Platform mounds at Moundville, Alabama, indicative of hierarchical Mississippian societies that dominated the Southeast from about 1000 to 1700.

c. 1100

The Chaco Canyon urban settlement in northwestern New Mexico is at its height.

The Mesa Verde site in southern Colorado is constructed.

1492–1600

As with the encounters between Norsemen and Inuits in Greenland and Newfoundland in the eleventh to the fourteenth centuries, there were probably other, intermittent contacts between Native Americans and Europeans before 1492.

Some Indians, most likely Inuit people, traveled east; two boats were shipwrecked in the Netherlands around 60 BC. Japanese sailors may have reached the coast of Ecuador around 5000 BC, and some scholars have suggested cultural similarities between the Chinese and Central American Indians from about 1000 BC. Other scholars have argued that North and West Africans may have contacted the Atlantic coasts of Central America between 1000 BC and AD 300, and possibly journeyed to Haiti, Panama, and Brazil between 1300 and 1450. European legend suggests that St. Brendan, an Irish priest and sailor, reached North America in AD 600. It is likely that between 1375 and 1491, Basque fishermen from northern Spain made brief encounters with the North American mainland as they tapped into the rich fishing areas off Cape Cod. Fishermen from Bristol may have done likewise between 1481 and 1491.

Whatever earlier contacts may have occurred, the arrival of Christopher Columbus in the Caribbean in 1492, and on three voyages during the following few

Left: A fanciful depiction of the landing of Christopher Columbus and his men in the Caribbean in 1492. Right: Vasco Nuñez de Balboa, who led an expedition across the Isthmus of Panama and reached the Pacific Ocean in 1513.

intensive labor to their new Spanish masters. The encomienda system required Indians to move to land owned by a Spanish man who held a grant from the Crown. Indian men typically had to work nine months out of the year on behalf of their Spanish masters. In effect, this amounted to slavery, since Indians were used to provide labor for individual Spaniards by mining, ranching, farming, or other public works. Despite the wording of the Laws of Burgos and renewed efforts at Christian conversion, much abuse of Indian people remained inherent to this labor system.

In addition to the encomienda system, Spain issued the *Requerimiento* in 1513, which was to be read to Indians as they were encountered throughout the Americas. The Requerimiento required Indians to accept the Catholic Church as the ruler of the world, and the monarchs of Spain as lords of their lands; in return, the Spanish would embrace them with open arms. If, however, Indians refused to heed this advice, the Requerimiento authorized Spanish forces to

Jean-Baptiste Debret's painting of a slave hunter in Brazil, c. 1840s.

1495–1496

European diseases on the Caribbean islands devastate Native populations, which had no prior exposure to the illnesses and therefore no immunity.

1497–1498

John and Sebastian Cabot voyage to "New-found-land" off the coast of eastern Canada. They establish contact with Native people.

wage war against Indians, forcibly convert them to Christianity, and enslave them. Since very few Indians understood Spanish, the Requerimiento acted more to justify Spanish seizure of Indian lands within Europe than to allow for constructive Spanish-Indian relations.

Spanish Invasion of North America

After the discovery of the immense mineral wealth of the Aztecan and Incan empires, Spanish military officers and government officials in the Americas realized that opportunities to become incomprehensively wealthy existed among some groups of Native peoples. Moreover, the Spanish believed that their conquest of the Aztecs and Incas proved their cultural and military superiority in the New World. Despite their arrogant faith in their own abilities, the

Left: Incan ritual vessel showing intricate design motifs and the gold material sought after by Europeans.

Right: Juan Ponce de León, colleague of Columbus and founder of Puerto Rico, searching for the fountain of youth.

Spanish had actually relied heavily on other Indian groups who were enemies of the Aztecs and Incas to provide thousands of soldiers in the fight against those powers. The use of Indian allies to fight against other Native groups and against other Europeans was adopted by all Europeans and then the American colonists to wage war. The initial Spanish forays into the North American Southwest and Southeast sometimes included armies of Indian allies in the search for the same riches that Cortés and the Pizarros had unearthed further south.

1500

Gaspar Corte-Real explores the northeastern coast.

1503

Abenakis and Passamaquoddies in Maine, along with other northeastern Indian groups, open trade with English and other European fishermen who travel annually to the area.

1506–1518

Huron and Iroquois groups along the St. Lawrence River in Canada open trade with French fishermen.

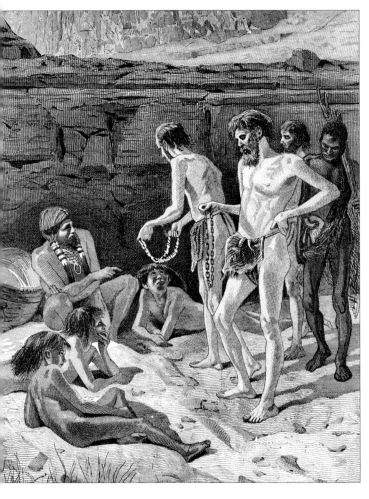

Cabeza de Vaca and companions, the only survivors of the Narváez expedition to Florida in the late 1520s.

Soon after the establishment of Hispaniola as a colony under Columbus, Spanish ships conducted slave raids on the Florida coasts. In 1513 and again in 1521, Juan Ponce de León, a member of Columbus's second expedition who had established the colony of Puerto Rico, tried to establish a colony in Florida. The Calusa Indians repelled these colonization attempts and killed Ponce de León. Although Spanish ships continued to prowl off the Atlantic and Gulf coasts of North America for many years, the next two major Spanish expeditions to North America and the opening of sustained direct contact between Indians and Europeans on the continent occurred back-to-back from 1526 to 1528. Throughout the first half of the sixteenth century, the Spanish who ventured to North America sought wealth along the lines of that discovered among the Aztecs and Incas, as well as Indian slaves to sell to the Caribbean plantations. Persistent rumors suggested that large, highly developed Native communities lived in the interior of North America. Lucas

Vázquez de Ayllón, a sugar planter on Hispaniola, led an expedition of around 500 colonists with supplies and livestock to the Atlantic coasts of Georgia and South Carolina in the summer of 1526. Within three months, Ayllón had died, and the surviving members of the colony turned back in the face of disease, lack of supplies, and hostility from local Indians. Only 150 survivors returned to Hispaniola.

In 1528, another expedition of about 400 men from Spain via Hispaniola journeyed to the Gulf of Florida under the leadership of Pánfilo de Narváez. Landing at Tampa Bay, the Narváez expedition traveled north and encountered the Timucuas and Apalachees of northern Florida. Relations between the Spanish and the Indians quickly became strained as violence occurred, trade proved fleeting, and little mineral wealth was found. The expedition members made it to the coast of the Florida corridor and built boats to sail back out into the Gulf of Mexico. Following the coast to the west, nearly eighty men washed up on shore in Galveston Bay in 1528 after a hurricane wrecked their boats. Over the next few years, the Spanish men and local Karankawa Indians died from diseases and

1512

The Laws of Burgos in Spain forbid the enslavement of Indians and establish the encomienda system.

1513

Juan Ponce de León explores Florida.

1519–1521

The Spanish under Hernán Cortés conquer the Aztec empire in central Mexico.

Acoma Pueblo in New Mexico, the oldest continuously inhabited city in the United States, founded c. 1200.

drought-induced starvation. In 1534, four survivors, including the famous chronicler Cabeza de Vaca and the slave Estevanico, traveled overland by foot from the coast of Texas through the Southwest and back to Spanish contact near Mexico City by 1536. They encountered and lived with several different Indian groups along their epic trek, and their information, despite the disastrous outcome of the Narváez expedition, inspired more Spanish journeys into the North American interior.

Spanish Invasion of the Southwest

Within a few years, an expedition was launched from Mexico City to present-day New Mexico. The Spanish sought the city of Cibola, which Estevanico and Cabeza de Vaca had heard of from Pima-speaking Ópatas in the northern Sonoran desert. Cibola was actually one of the Zuni pueblos of New Mexico and was reported to be rich in turquoise and other precious stones. Spanish officials in Mexico City assumed Cibola was one of the "seven cities of gold" reputed to exist somewhere in the Americas. An initial exploratory party under Fray Marcos de Niza and guided by Estevanico, the Narváez

c. 1520

The first epidemics of European diseases hit North America.

1521

The Calusas on the Florida coast resist Spanish attempts to establish a colony.

Juan Ponce de León again explores the coasts of Florida.

men were traveling about. Cabrillo's forces moved farther north up the coast to Santa Catalina Island and wintered among the Gabrielino Indians there. The Indians killed Cabrillo in an attack, but the Spanish soldiers apparently stayed in the region and intermarried with the Indians. In the 1560s, the Spanish again became interested in California as a base to protect their fleets traveling from Central and South America to the Philippines. Spanish ships stopped along the California coast to get fresh food and water, and to trade with Indians such as the Pomos, Miwoks, and Chumash. Sir Francis Drake arrived from England and traded with the Miwoks in 1579, but the English failed to establish a colony. Little additional contact between Californian Indians and Europeans occurred during the next 150 years.

Spanish Invasion of the Southeast

After the failure of the Narváez expedition in the late 1520s, the Spanish did not make further

At Chumash Painted Cave, California, sacred symbols and mnemonic devices tell stories about the Chumash past.

1533

The Pizarro brothers conquer the Incan empire.

1534

Cabeza de Vaca, Estevanico, and the two other survivors of the Narváez expedition set out from Texas to Mexico.

French explorer Jacques Cartier seizes two Iroquois men and takes them to France.

forays into the Southeast until the expedition of Hernando de Soto entered the western coast of Florida at Tampa Bay in 1539. De Soto had taken part as an officer in Francisco and Gonzalo Pizarro's Peruvian expedition against the Incas earlier in the decade, which had made him one of the richest Spaniards in Nicaragua, and also a governing official. He sought his own colony in the New World in order to amass the tremendous wealth and power he witnessed among the Incas. Although partly concerned with converting Indians to Christianity, de Soto intended to find gold, and to take Indian slaves to serve in his new colony. He amassed a force of more than 500 soldiers, dozens of horses and war dogs (mastiffs and Irish wolfhounds), and hundreds of pigs to act as a mobile food source. After landing in Tampa Bay, de Soto's expedition found a Spanish survivor from the Narváez expedition, Juan Ortiz, who had been living among Indians in Florida for twelve years. Ortiz acted as a translator between de Soto's forces and the Indians in central Florida. Along

Queen Elizabeth of England knighting Sir Francis Drake in 1581.

1534–1542

Cartier explores the coast of Labrador and the St. Lawrence River, and attempts to establish a colony.

1535–1536

Cartier establishes contact and trade with Iroquoian groups at Stadacona (Quebec) and Hochelaga (Montreal).

The landing of Hernando de Soto and his forces at Tampa Bay in 1539. De Soto's men traveled throughout the Southeast for three years, unleashing destruction and diseases.

1536

The Hochelagans teach Jacque Cartier's men how to cure scurvy by brewing white cedar tea rich in vitamin C.

Iroquois chief Donnacona assists Cartier in exploring the St. Lawrence River valley and accompanies Cartier back to France.

c. 1539

Donnacona dies in France.

the way, multilingual Indians were kidnapped by the expedition so that translations from Spanish through Ortiz and a string of Indian interpreters would enable de Soto to communicate with the Indian groups he encountered, at least partially. At first, de Soto's men were encouraged by the small amounts of gold they discovered among Indians in central Florida, not knowing that the gold came from Spanish shipwrecks that had been rummaged through by coastal Indians and then traded to the interior. Slowly, de Soto's forces traveled north, since they were told by nearly every Indian society they encountered over the next four years that the gold and other riches they sought could be found among the neighboring people a few days' travel away.

De Soto's expedition entered the world of Mississippian chiefdoms that characterized the Southeast at this time. At many of the Mississippian villages, caciques, or chiefs, were carried on stretchers on the shoulders of their men and exercised authoritarian power. At the chiefdom of Cofitachequi in present-day South Carolina, the primary chief was a woman. De Soto took advantage of this hierarchical political structure by kidnapping chiefs and demanding

that their followers pay ransom in foodstuffs, rare minerals, women, and slaves. Some Mississippian groups already knew to be fearful of the Spanish due to their past experiences with, or knowledge of, previous expeditions. Other Mississippians wanted to use the Spanish to help them fight against their Native enemies. De Soto took advantage of the rivalries among neighboring Mississippian groups, as the Spanish had done in defeating the Aztecs and Incas, and tried to get their assistance in intimidating other chiefdoms. As the weeks and months dragged on, de Soto's forces found increasing resistance among each chiefdom they encountered as word of the Spanish expedition spread through the Southeast. De Soto's army often had to attack and plunder villages for food supplies, and to seize slaves and concubines. Although Spanish weapons—along with their horses and war dogs—outgunned the Indians, de Soto's men suffered increasingly larger losses at the hands of the chiefdoms. In a well-planned attack at the Battle of Mabila in 1540, the chiefdom of

Wa-Na-Ta, a chief of the Dakota Sioux, in traditional buffalo-skin clothing and with his European-made gun.

1539

Francisco de Coronado's expedition encounters violent resistance from pueblos in New Mexico.

Estevanico, the survivor of the Narváez expedition, leads Coronado's forces to the Zuni pueblos and is killed by the Zunis.

Hernando de Soto's expedition lands at Tampa Bay with 500 soldiers, dozens of horses, and hundreds of pigs.

Chief William Riding In, probably Pawnee, with a bear claw necklace, c. 1932.

Tazcaluza killed twenty-two Spaniards and wounded 148, although a thousand or so Indians also died. This episode marked a turning point in de Soto's expedition as his forces licked their wounds, wintered among the Chickasaws in northern Mississippi, and then crossed the Mississippi River in 1541. By that point, de Soto and his men sought to return to Mexico, since their supplies were gone and the hoped-for riches had not materialized. While searching for signs of Spanish settlements in Texas, de Soto's forces unknowingly came within a few hundred miles of Coronado's expedition, which had reached Kansas around the same time. De Soto died in 1542 and his men sunk his body in the Mississippi River in a futile attempt to hide his death from neighboring Indians; de Soto had claimed to be a child of the sun, the ultimate expression of power for Mississippian Indians. The surviving Spanish soldiers built boats and set off down the Mississippi River in 1543. There they encountered large fleets of boats with hundreds of Indians who fought against them

all the way to the Gulf of Mexico. Eventually, several survivors reached Mexico City and transcribed the history of the expedition.

After the failure of de Soto's expedition, the Spanish did not return to the Southeast until the colonizing expedition of Tristán de Luna landed at Pensacola in 1559. De Luna was accompanied by a thousand settlers, their wives, children, missionaries, African slaves, Mexican Indians, and a Coosa chiefdom woman who had been captured by the de Soto expedition. Indian groups along and near the coast fled before the Spanish, but the Coosas of northern Alabama welcomed the Spanish as allies in their fight against a neighboring chiefdom. The Coosas could not feed the large Spanish contingent over the long term, however, and in 1560 the Spanish abandoned yet another attempt to settle in the Southeast.

The village of San Agustín (St. Augustine) was established on the Atlantic coast of Florida under Don Pedro Menéndez de Avilés in 1565. As with the Spanish return to California in the 1560s, the purpose of the new settlement in Florida centered on protecting Spanish shipping routes for the gold and silver galleons that voyaged from Central America to Spain each year, and to

1539-1542

The de Soto expedition finds Juan Ortiz, a survivor of the earlier Narváez expedition, and employs him as an interpreter.

Coronado leads a doomed expedition to the Southwest in search of the mythical "seven cities of gold."

De Soto leads an ill-fated expedition to the Southeast in search of riches, and encounters sharp resistance from Mississippian Indian societies.

destroy a fledgling French colony that had been established in the same area the year before. San Agustín became primarily a military garrison designed to protect Spanish interests in the Caribbean and Central America, rather than a settlement that attempted to enslave Indians or find mineral wealth. The Spanish in San Agustín traded with Indians, particularly for food, and San Agustín served as a base for the development and expansion of the Catholic mission system among Indians in northern and central Florida, and also along the coasts of Georgia and the Carolinas.

Another Spanish expedition, led by Juan Pardo, arrived on the South Carolina coast in 1566, seeking to extend a string of forts deep into the North American interior. Pardo and his forces journeyed to the Cofitachequi chiefdom that had been sacked by de Soto a quarter-century earlier and found a much-reduced population there. Pardo's men wintered with the neighboring Joara chiefdom, which had been a dependency of Cofitachequi in the early 1540s,

Depiction of Indian slaves loading gold onto Spanish galleons in Panama.

1540

The Battle of Mabila is waged between the Hernando de Soto expedition and Mississippian Indians in lower Alabama. Nearly a thousand Indian men and two dozen Spaniards die.

Chief Tuskaloosa leads thousands of Indians in a surprise attack on de Soto's Spanish forces at Mabila.

De Soto's men seize the Lady of Cofitachequi, the leader of a chiefdom in the Carolinas.

and then continued west in the spring of 1567. They turned back just before reaching the Coosa chiefdom that had been encountered by both the de Soto and the de Luna expeditions, and retreated back to the coast on the rumor that the Coosas intended to attack this new group of Spanish intruders. Spanish efforts to colonize the eastern North American interior now ended.

Spanish Missions in the Southeast

After establishing the first permanent settlements around San Agustín, Spanish attention turned toward peaceful relations with Indians and converting them to Catholicism. Missionaries and the missions themselves became the agent of Spanish control over the Indians in Florida and surrounding areas. Eventually, the Spanish established a string of missions set among the Timucuas, Guales, and Apalachees across northern Florida and up the Atlantic coast. In 1566 Franciscans established the missions of Santa Elena and Santa Catalina among the Guale Indians on the Georgian

A depiction of the Timucua Indians of Florida preparing for war against a rival tribe.

1542

Hernando de Soto dies and is buried in the Mississippi River.

The New Laws of the Indies require the Catholic Church to intensify conversion efforts among American Indians.

Luis de Alvarado Moscoso assumes command of the de Soto expedition and leads it westward into Red River country, encountering the Caddos.

Ruins that are said to be part of a former Spanish mission on the coast of Georgia.

coast. The missionaries worked to undermine Native religion while ingratiating themselves among their Native hosts. In the Guale villages, the Franciscans replaced dance poles in sacred grounds with crosses, which became new symbols of spiritual power. The missionaries converted the village council houses to chapels, which mimicked Guale custom, since each was a public space where people met to discuss the concerns of the community. Finally, the missionaries focused on the village chiefs in the hope that other villagers would follow their examples and convert. The Franciscans enjoyed relative success until the Guale Indians revolted against the Spanish in 1597. The revolt targeted the priests specifically because they had tried to prevent matrilineal succession and name their own new chiefs. The missionaries also opposed polygamy, which angered their closest converts among chiefs and other elite men, who traditionally viewed having more than one wife as a sign of high status. The Guale revolt took eight years for the Spanish to put down and forever destroyed the Guale missions. The Spanish separated "Christian" Indians from "pagan" Indians after this point, and the Christian Indians lived in or near Spanish settlements such as San Agustín. Additional missions were established among the Timucuas at Mocama on present-day Cumberland Island in 1587.

The Spanish also attempted to set up a mission among the Powhatan Indians of Virginia in 1570. Spanish ships had entered Chesapeake Bay for decades, and one of them kidnapped a Powhatan boy in 1561, converted him to Christianity, renamed him Don Luis, and then carried him to Spain, Mexico, and Cuba throughout the next decade. He escorted eight Jesuit missionaries and a young boy from Cuba to Virginia in 1570. Don Luis soon abandoned his Spanish comrades, and his people killed the missionaries, except for one young boy. A Spanish retaliatory force arrived in

Puritan missionary John Eliot converted many Indians to Christianity in New England.

1543

A Spanish expedition lands at the site of San Diego, California, and explores the California coastline.

Moscoso leads the de Soto expedition back to the Mississippi River, and eventually down that river, and then back to Mexico.

traded with Indians along the coasts and into the St. Lawrence River. In the last two decades of the sixteenth century, the rendezvous point of Tadoussac, at the confluence of the St. Lawrence and Saguenay rivers, became a major point of French-Indian interaction. Algonquian peoples, such as the Montagnais and Algonkins, controlled this exchange site to the exclusion of Iroquoians, for example the Five Nations Iroquois and the Hurons. European goods— metal products, glass beads, and copper materials—entered the Northeast at Tadoussac and the centuries-long fur trade between the French and Indian peoples of the North was begun. The new goods sparked intense competition among Native peoples for access to, and control over, high-status trade items. Around this time, the villages of Stadacona and Hochelaga were abandoned, with their residents most likely joining either the Five Nations Iroquois or the Hurons. The reason for the movement may have stemmed from the increasing power of their enemy, the

An engraving of a print depicting Indian hunting techniques, by Jacques Le Moyne de Morgues.

1560–1570

Don Luis visits Mexico, Spain, and Cuba.

1563

The French establish Fort Caroline on Florida's northeastern coast.

Frenchman Jacques Le Moyne de Morgues draws a series of popular representations of Indians living near Fort Caroline in Florida.

Algonquians, or because disease weakened the inhabitants and encouraged the survivors to seek safety among distant relatives.

In the early 1560s, France tried to establish a colony on the Atlantic coast of northern Florida. In 1562 Admiral Gaspard de Coligny and navigator Jean Ribault left twenty-eight men on present-day Parris Island in Port Royal Sound to build a fort, intending to establish a colony there. Troubled by starvation and Indian attacks, these men abandoned the colony within a year. In 1564 a colonizing effort led by René Goulaine de Laudonnière brought nearly 200 settlers to St. John's Bluff in northern Florida, where they constructed Fort Caroline. In June 1565, Ribault returned with hundreds of additional soldiers and colonists, and took command of the fledgling colony. However, Spanish forces under the rule of Don Pedro Menéndez de Avilés attacked the colony in 1565 and killed nearly all of the men. The Spanish then established San Agustín and fought back subsequent French attempts to dislodge them from the region. Although Fort Caroline was a failure as a colony, two of the Frenchmen who survived left an enduring record of these events and of the Indian people they encountered in the region. The drawings and paintings of Jacques Le Moyne de Morgues remain one of the best early visual records of the area's Timucua Indian people and its flora and fauna. The French commander Laudonnière wrote a history of his experiences in the region, including interactions with Indian people.

The English and the Roanoke Colony

During the sixteenth century, Indians along the coast of North Carolina had occasionally encountered Europeans shipwrecked on the Outer Banks. In 1558, for example, the Secotans helped a Spanish crew to rebuild a boat so they could return to Florida. In 1584 an English explorer named Arthur Barlowe arrived on the Outer Banks and immediately began planning to establish a colony. Barlowe took two local Roanoke Indian men, Manteo and Wanchese, back to England to help promote the colony. Barlowe's employer, Sir Walter Raleigh, became convinced of the possibility of a successful colony and dispatched a company of soldiers and settlers to the region in 1585. Arriving with Manteo and Wanchese, the colonists' relations

Sir Walter Raleigh, who financed the attempt by England to establish a colony on the coast of North Carolina in the 1580s.

1565

The Spanish at St. Augustine develop trade for food with Indian people nearby.

The Spanish, under the rule of Don Pedro Menéndez de Avilés, establish St. Augustine and Santa Elena in Florida, and then destroy the French presence in the area.

Spanish Jesuit missionary efforts begin among the Calusas.

with the Indians began amicably. Tensions erupted when a local Indian chief was accused of stealing an English cup, and the colonists responded by burning his village and all of its food stores to the ground. The Roanokes and other neighboring Indians then refused to voluntarily provide the English with food. The colony's military commander, Ralph Lane, called a peace conference in the summer of 1586, at which the English assassinated the Roanoke chief, Wingina. From that moment, despite the efforts of Raleigh to send additional settlers and soldiers to the colony, Indians in the area refused to cooperate with the English. When a relief force arrived in 1587 under John White, it took revenge on a group of Croatoan Indians on Cape Hatteras, mistakenly attacking the one Native group in the area still friendly with the English. White was sent back to England for additional supplies, but, because of the attack of the Spanish Armada on England in 1588, he was unable to return until 1590. By then, the colony had been abandoned—the only clue to

Algonquian Indians of North Carolina performing a dance and religious ritual, c. 1590.

1566–1568

Juan Pardo conducts two expeditions from Santa Elena into the interior of the Southeast.

1570

The Spanish attempt to establish a mission among the Powhatans on the Chesapeake Bay, but the Powhatans kill all the missionaries, except for a young boy.

Don Luis leads a Spanish mission to Chesapeake Bay before rejoining his people and allowing them to kill the Spaniards.

the colonists' whereabouts was the word "Croatoan" carved into a tree. The Roanoke colonists may have joined the Croatoans or another Indian group or they may have been killed, though direct evidence for either interpretation was never found. White never again saw his daughter and granddaughter, who had been among the colonists he left in 1587. However, he and fellow colonist Thomas Hariot left a rich visual and written record of the Indians of coastal Carolina in paintings and books published after their return to England.

The Impact of European Diseases

The first century of European contact with North America had far-reaching repercussions for the Indian people of California, the Southwest, Southeast, Atlantic seaboard, and Northeast. Hundreds of Indians had died in open violence between the peoples, but nothing caused a greater impact on the continent than disease. European contact set off chain reactions of diseases throughout the regions where Europeans set foot. Europeans and their livestock carried a host of new microbes to the Americas for the first time,

Algonquian Indians of the mid-Atlantic coast, treating their sick with herbal medicines and spiritual assistance, c. 1591.

1572

Spanish Jesuit missionaries leave Florida after several of them are killed by Indians.

1573

The Spanish Pacification Ordinance forbids the military conquest of Native people.

Spanish Franciscan missionaries arrive in Florida.

shell-shocked survivors to pick up the pieces and start again from scratch. Oral traditions, sacred understandings, and medical knowledge sometimes vanished with the elders as well. All of this occurred at the same time that new political and economic pressures and opportunities were being exerted upon Indians, creating what some have aptly called an Indians' New World.

The Collapse of the Mississippian World

The deadliest killer by far was smallpox, and the area in North America that suffered the greatest degree of change in the sixteenth century due to the disease was the Southeast. Scholars disagree about whether or not Hernando de Soto's expedition in the early 1540s introduced smallpox, but there is little doubt that massive changes occurred throughout the region shortly after the remnants of his group escaped into the Gulf of Mexico. De Soto's expedition may have introduced smallpox and other diseases via

Lacrosse is a sport that was passed on from the Iroquois and other Native peoples to Canadians and Americans.

1582

Pueblo Indians kill the Franciscan missionaries left behind by the Rodríguez expedition.

Spaniard Antonio de Espejo leads an expedition to New Mexico.

sick troops or the hundreds of pigs that accompanied the army. Nearly all of the Mississippian chiefdoms that existed when de Soto visited the region collapsed shortly afterward. Political and military power among the region's Indian societies became diffused and scattered. War and fighting against the Spanish, as at the Battle of Mabila in 1540, could account for localized political and demographic changes, but not for the region-wide collapse that happened. Later, Spanish explorers in the 1560s, such as the de Luna expedition, found many of the chiefdom towns mentioned by the de Soto chroniclers nearly deserted or abandoned, and the chiefdoms still in existence seemed smaller and less capable of ruling over satellite communities. When French explorers journeyed down the Mississippi River over a century later in the 1680s, they found only a small fraction of the villages and chiefdoms that had once put hundreds of canoes in the Mississippi River in an attempt to attack the remnants of de Soto's forces. Although reduced in size, a few Mississippian chiefdoms persisted, the most famous being the Natchez chiefdom on the east bank of the lower Mississippi River.

Left: Me-Na-Wa, a Creek war leader of the early nineteenth century.

Right: Spaniard Juan Pardo explored the Carolinas and Tennessee, and met with Indian groups in 1566–68.

1584

Englishman Arthur Barlowe arrives among the Roanokes on the Outer Banks of North Carolina.

1585–1590

The English attempt to establish a colony among Native peoples such as the Roanokes and Croatoans at Roanoke Island on the North Carolina coast.

Indian opposition to the English Roanoke colony dooms the settlement. The fate of its English survivors remains unknown.

1600–1700

After the fleeting interactions between Indians and Europeans in sixteenth-century North America, the seventeenth century brought about changes that saw a period of more sustained contact.

The establishment of more European colonies and the arrival of thousands of Europeans on the continent created new issues and points of contention between Europeans and Indians, while simultaneously exacerbating already-existing conditions of disease, warfare, and trade. Several wars between Europeans and Indians—and among various Indian groups against each other—erupted in the seventeenth

century as a result of more aggressive European colonization. The Indian response to sustained European colonization ranged from resistance to cooperation to opportunistic geopolitical maneuvering.

French-Indian Relations

In 1603 French explorer and colonizer Samuel de Champlain sailed the same route up the St. Lawrence River that Jacques Cartier had traveled seventy years earlier. Although he explored the same path, Champlain saw a very different Native world: there were no fields of corn, no villages, and few people along the river. The Iroquoian peoples who had lived at Stadacona and Hochelaga had

Left: A painting of the "first Thanksgiving" shows pilgrims feeding Massasoit's Wampanoag Indians. Right: French explorer Samuel de Champlain, who explored the St. Lawrence River Valley and Lake Champlain in the early seventeenth century.

An Indian encampment on Lake Huron in the nineteenth century. French traders initiated trade with Indians throughout the Great Lakes region in the seventeenth century.

abandoned the area due to diseases and warfare with other Indians. Champlain founded Quebec City, and French traders soon developed a working relationship with the Hurons, who lived further west, and the Algonquins and Montagnais, who lived to the east. These groups quickly monopolized trade with the French and became middlemen by requiring other tribes to trade with them in order to get European goods. The Hurons likewise prevented the French from expanding into the interior and reaching other western tribes for trade. The Hurons, Algonquins, and Montagnais sought close relations with the French for economic and political reasons. French tradegoods enhanced their status and power relative to tribes who did not maintain direct trade with the French.

Guns and Warfare

France's support for its Huron and various Algonquian allies caused conflicts with other tribes, especially the Five Nations Iroquois. In 1609 Champlain led a small French scouting party, accompanied by Algonquins and Hurons, south across what is now Lake Champlain. There he encountered a group of Mohawks (one

1600

The Spanish in the Southwest kidnap Apaches, Navajos, and Utes to exploit as slave labor.

1601

The Spanish crush the Guale revolt.

1602

May 15 Englishman Bartholomew Gosnold explores Cape Cod and encounters Indian people there.

The Wichitas acquire horses.

of the five tribes of the Iroquois Confederacy) in canoes. The two groups of Indians exchanged insults and then journeyed to the shore, lining up in ranks for a ritual battle. They lobbed arrows at each other, and individuals ran between the two groups to taunt the opposing force and show their bravery.

Champlain and other Frenchmen decided to assist their Huron and Algonquin allies by introducing a deadly new element into this ritualized form of warfare. They fired their muskets and killed several Mohawk chiefs, scaring the rest into fleeing. In so doing, Champlain made lifelong enemies of the Iroquois who were already angered at French dealings with the Hurons. Warfare changed forever in the Northeast as the Iroquois demanded guns from this point on. The Mohawks eagerly opened trade with the Dutch in New Amsterdam (Albany) after 1614, in order to circumvent the French trade with their enemies by controlling their own access to European guns and other supplies. Once Indians in the Northeast had acquired guns, they abandoned fighting in ranks out in the open, along with the use of wooden armor that stopped arrows, and small-scale raids (so-called

....

Left: An Iowa Indian, from around the nineteenth century, wearing both Native and European clothing, indicative of the impact of trade with Europeans.

Right: An Iroquois warrior scalping a captive.

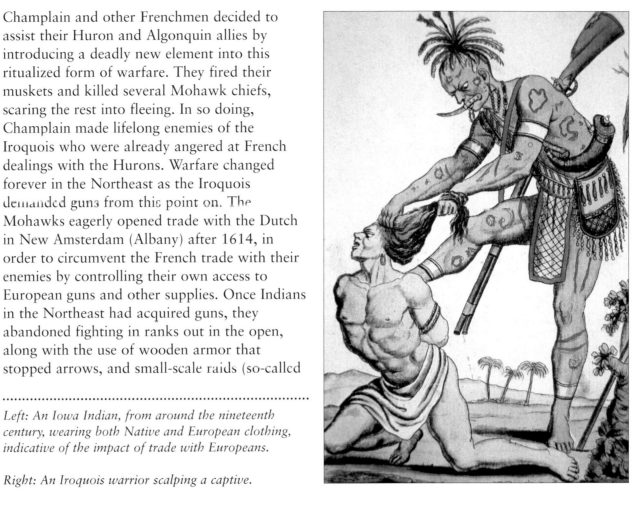

1603

Englishman Martin Pring explores the New England coast.

Indian warfare) become their preferred method of attack. Throughout North America, Indian peoples made similar adjustments as either they or their neighbors obtained guns, and warfare became far more frequent and deadly.

Trade, Missions, and Intermarriage

In the seventeenth century, France set up a chain of trading posts from the Great Lakes all the way down the Mississippi River to New Orleans. This thin line of French posts hemmed in the English colonies being established to the east and theoretically prevented their expansion, but the encirclement really rested on Indian allies and maintaining trade relations with Indian people. French power in North America depended on their ability to get along with various Indian groups. From 1673 to 1674, fur trader Louis Joliet and Catholic priest Jacques Marquette canoed down the Fox, Wisconsin, and Mississippi rivers, confirming that the Mississippi emptied into the Gulf of Mexico. The person most responsible for extending France's claims in the interior of North America was René-Robert Cavelier, Sieur de La Salle, who led expeditions throughout the Great

A scene reminiscent of frontier trading posts where Indians and Europeans came together to trade.

1603–1615

Frenchman Samuel de Champlain explores the Northeast and establishes trade contacts with various Algonquian and Iroquoian peoples.

Champlain discovers that Stadacona and Hochelaga have been abandoned by the Iroquois, perhaps because European diseases have depleted the population or because of war between the Iroquois and other Native peoples in the region.

Lakes area, to the Ohio River, and down the Mississippi River. He constructed Fort Frontenac on Lake Ontario in 1673, Fort Conti at the mouth of the Niagara River in 1679, Fort Miami in Michigan in 1680, and Fort Crèvecoeur in Illinois in 1681. In 1682 La Salle, along with a party of Frenchmen and Indians, canoed down the Mississippi River, establishing Fort Prudhomme at present-day Memphis, Tennessee, and reaching the mouth of the Mississippi River. From 1684 to 1687, he attempted to establish a colony on the Gulf of Mexico along the coast of Texas, but he was killed by his men and the colony failed. In 1699 French forces led by Pierre Le Moyne, Sieur d'Iberville, reached Ship Island off the coast of Biloxi, Mississippi, and established a permanent colony on the Gulf Coast near an existing Indian village. With that encounter, the French presence in the South was established, and French-Indian interaction and trade began. From the beginning, the Louisiana colony was plagued by food and provision shortages, and the French had to rely on food provided by Indians.

The French had to strive constantly to maintain good relations with Indians. Relatively

few French people came to settle in North America during the seventeenth century; only about 2,000 French citizens lived in the St. Lawrence River valley in the 1660s. French success in North America during the seventeenth century and later depended heavily on the fur trade and on strong alliances with various Indian groups. The French in North America usually abided by Indian rules of diplomacy in order to smooth relations and facilitate trade. Diplomatic rituals included smoking the calumet pipe, offering gifts, and engaging in hours (and sometimes days) of negotiations.

French Catholic missionaries provided another key element of French-Indian relations. Jesuit priests fanned out among Indian communities in northeastern North America, seeking Indian converts. Preaching first among the Abenakis and Algonquins, Father Jean de Brébeuf led the Jesuits to the Huron villages north of Lake Ontario in 1634. The Hurons resisted Jesuit interference within their villages

French-Canadian explorer Pierre Le Moyne, Sieur d'Iberville, who established the French settlement of the lower Mississippi valley in the early seventeenth century.

c. 1605

Penobscot Abenaki leader Bashebes heads a confederation of Indian communities.

1605

Englishman George Waymouth explores the coast of Maine.

The Spanish reopen the Guale missions.

Left: A depiction of a meeting between French officials and Iroquois Indians.

Right: Kateri Tekakwitha, the Mohawk woman who survived smallpox and is considered a saint by many Catholics.

die from smallpox, which had also left her physically scarred, and she embraced Catholicism and a life of service. On her death in 1680 at the age of twenty-four, her scars apparently disappeared. Pilgrims began visiting her shrine, and the Catholic Church began the process of conferring sainthood on her.

The coming together of different cultures in North America produced a cultural and religious contest between Indians and Europeans as each tried to convert the other. Christianity is an exclusive religion and generally does not allow adoption of other beliefs, whereas Native American religions were often more inclusive, and people were willing to adopt other beliefs and incorporate them into

and therefore killed some priests, but generally the Jesuits exerted minimal pressure on Indian communities to adopt French ways. The Jesuits also accepted partial conversions to Catholicism among their Indian followers. Some Indian people, such as the Mohawk woman Kateri Tekakwitha, converted completely to Catholicism. Tekakwitha saw her entire family

1606

Spanish Franciscans establish missions among the Timucuas in central Florida.

French Jesuits establish the settlement of De Poutrincourt at Port Royal, Nova Scotia.

1607

May 14 The English Virginia Company establishes Jamestown colony among the Powhatans.

June 14 The English Plymouth Company establishes Popham colony (or Sagadahoc) in Maine.

their own. Christian missionaries such as French Jesuits sought a social and religious revolution in Indian societies. In order to be effective, they had to undermine the power of Indian religious leaders. The influx of diseases often helped in this effort, since the Indian people's faith in shamans sometimes diminished when diseases could not be cured by traditional means. In the midst of chaos and great changes, Indians reacted in different ways to missionaries: some adopted the new religion and world view as an answer to their problems, some admitted that the European religions must have power because of European technology and immunity to diseases, others insisted that their religion and way of life was superior, and some reacted violently to missionary efforts.

French Catholic missionaries usually went to live among Indian groups and sought to convert Indians first and then to "civilize" them into French society. Jesuits learned Indian languages and insisted that Indian people could keep much of their culture and still become Christian.

A painting by Paul Kane of Canadian Indians in the nineteenth century, probably on the Pacific coast.

1608

The French establish Quebec and the settlement quickly becomes a center of trade between the French and Algonquian peoples in the Northeast.

1609–1614

The Powhatans and the English fight a protracted war in Virginia, and hundreds are killed. The war ends with the English capture of Pocahontas, the daughter of Powhatan chief Wahunsonacock.

Catholic rituals and symbolism appealed to many Indians because their religious practices also called for ceremonies and ritual objects. A group of Pennacock Indians told English missionaries in 1700 that they preferred the French, "for the French gave them silver crosses to wear on their necks." French Jesuits took up the lifestyles of their Indian hosts and often immersed themselves in Native society; some even became accepted enough to represent the tribe at negotiations with colonial officials. Consequently, French missionaries converted many more Indians than their English competitors in the Northeast. However, French Jesuits also caused divisions in Indian societies because they were in direct competition with Indian religious leaders, and converted Indians were often forced to live in villages separate from those of their unconverted kinfolk.

Intermarriage between French traders and Indian women further facilitated good relations between the two peoples. French traders often acted on their own authority and traveled deep into the continent, seeking beaver furs that brought a profit in the European market, and relied solely on Indian allies, wives, and relatives

for protection. Having Indian relatives meant that a trader had obligations to provide them goods, and they had obligations to protect his merchandise. Indian people often viewed kinship relations as more important than tribal or racial affiliations, and French fur traders brought their Native families prestige and power. In some parts of North America, particularly along today's U.S.-Canadian border area west of the Great Lakes, new people called *metis,* part French and part Indian, arose and formed unique communities that persist to this day.

The Iroquois

No Indian group exerted as much power and influence over Europeans and other Indians in seventeenth-century North America than the Haudenosaunee (People of the Longhouse), known also as the Iroquois League. *Iroquois* was an Algonquian Indian term meaning "snake" or "enemy" and was the first name that the French learned for these people. The Five Nations, as the Iroquois were also called,

A painting purporting to be of Shikellamy, the Oneida (Iroquois) chieftain.

1609

Huron and Algonquian groups ally with France against the Five Nations Iroquois.

July Samuel de Champlain, with Algonquian and Montagnais allies, clashes with Mohawk Iroquois, and his men use firearms to kill Mohawk chiefs.

Henry Hudson explores New England and the Hudson River.

were composed of the Senecas, Cayugas, Onondagas, Oneidas, and Mohawks.

In Iroquois legend, a woman named Aataentsic fell through a hole in the sky and landed on the back of a sea turtle. She gathered dirt and planted seeds while bringing all of the animals together on her new land, otherwise known as North America or "Turtle Island." The story of how the Iroquois League was created is no less remarkable, but it occurred later. The creation of the league is believed to have taken place sometime in the fifteenth century, before European contact but following a long period of civil war between the five tribes and the culturally related Hurons. Two heroes, an Onondaga man named Hiawatha and a Huron man named Deganawidah ("the Great Peacemaker"), established peace and unity among the five nations. They traveled around the villages of the five nations and convinced the Iroquois to meet together and create a new government that would preserve peace while simultaneously empowering the Iroquois groups.

....

A romanticized painting of the Onondaga (Iroquois) hero Hiawatha sitting with his wife.

1610

Dutchman Adrien Block explores the New England coast and encounters Indian people.

The Spanish establish Santa Fe in the Southwest.

A portrait of an Iroquois woman, c. 1900. Iroquois women controlled agriculture and families.

The five nations created a confederacy that preserved each member's individual autonomy except in matters of foreign policy. The Senecas, whose villages were located the farthest west in western New York and were the most populous, became the "keepers of the western door," charged with protecting the confederacy from enemies in the Great Lakes area to the west. The Mohawks became known as the "keepers of the eastern door," guarding against any enemy incursions from the east. Each tribe had an equal vote in confederacy meetings. The Iroquois held all confederacy-wide council meetings among the Onondagas, whose villages were located in the geographical center of the confederacy and who, as the home of Hiawatha, provided the spiritual and political center of the confederacy. Each tribe sent civil chiefs appointed by clan mothers to the councils at Onondaga, and women played crucial political roles in selecting chiefs, determining whether or not to go to war, and deciding the fates of any captives seized in war from other peoples. Representatives of almost every Iroquois clan—named after founding animals such as the turtle, wolf, bear, beaver, deer, or hawk—could be found in each village. Ancestry and clan identification came through the mother's line, making the Iroquois a matrilineal society. Clan mothers were the highest-ranking members of each clan, and women controlled the households, the fields (where they grew corn, beans, and squash), and access to the family through adoption. At council meetings the Onondagas sent fourteen civil chiefs, the Mohawks nine, the Senecas eight, the Cayugas nine, and the Oneidas ten, making a total of fifty, but one Onondaga seat was left vacant in honor of Hiawatha. Unanimity was required for any decision, but clan mothers could override any decision to go to war. If a particular village or tribe did not agree with the consensual decision, they could leave and form a new community with little controversy, as was the case for many Iroquois who moved westward and south into the Ohio valley and became known as Mingos.

War Against the Hurons and Algonquins

One decision that the Iroquois League made in the early 1640s was to wage war on their Huron and Algonquian neighbors. In a series of large-scale attacks over several years, the

1614

January 30 Pocahontas and Rolfe have a son, Thomas, who returns to Virginia and carries on his mother's bloodline.

Patuxet Indian Squanto, together with twenty-three other Natives, is taken prisoner by English captain Thomas Hunt on the coast of New England, and sold into slavery in Spain.

The Dutch establish a presence on the Hudson River near Albany and open a lucrative trade with Indians.

April 5 Pocahontas converts to Christianity and marries English colonist John Rolfe.

A battle between Europeans and their Indian allies against other Indians, indicative of the world of war created by European settlement of North America.

Iroquois wiped out numerous Huron and other Indian villages. Since many of these Indian groups were also allied with the French, the Iroquois sometimes attacked French settlements. By the mid-seventeenth century, the Iroquois were the dominant military power in northeastern North America, and had extended their reach from the Hudson River to the Great Lakes and from the Ohio valley to the St. Lawrence River. One scholarly interpretation of these attacks calls this era of violence the "Beaver Wars," which emphasizes the Iroquois desire to eliminate competitors who traded beaver skins to the French for guns and other products. The Iroquois sought their own unfettered access to guns and other European trade items. The Mohawks established a trade with the Dutch along the Hudson River from the 1620s to the 1660s in order to circumvent the French trade, while the Senecas and other Iroquois groups wanted to prevent their Huron and western Algonquian neighbors from becoming too powerful. A more recent interpretation of the wars waged from the 1640s by the Iroquois on their neighbors is that they were engaged in "Mourning Wars" and sought

1616

June Pocahontas travels to England with her husband John Rolfe, but dies before returning to Virginia.

1616–1619

A series of smallpox epidemics strikes Indians in New England.

Peter Minuit, director-general of the Dutch colony of New Netherland, buying Manhattan Island from the Canarsee Indians.

captives to adopt into their families and society. The Iroquois population, which had been around 12,000 in 1650, was falling in the late seventeenth century because of diseases and warfare. They therefore replaced deceased relatives with women and children seized from other groups; adult male captives usually suffered torture and death. France sent regular troops to Canada in the 1660s to wage war on the Iroquois, and the Iroquois lost a trading partner when the Dutch relinquished the New Netherland colony to the English at the same time. The Iroquois established a formal relationship with the English in the 1670s, but that connection pulled them into wars between France and England. The Iroquois League tried to prevent further population loss by appealing for peace with the French in 1698 and declaring in 1701, in the aftermath of King William's War, that they would remain neutral in all future conflicts between their European neighbors rather than lose more men to the fighting.

Powhatan-English Relations in Virginia

Another powerful Indian group greeted the English who arrived to establish Jamestown in

1618

Tobacco becomes the major source of profit in Virginia, requiring access to Indian land.

Powhatan paramount chief Wahunsonacock dies. He is succeeded by his brother and primary Powhatan war leader, Opechancanough.

1619

A Patuxet Indian named Squanto returns to New England after spending time in Spain, and then with English merchant John Slaney, who sent him home with Newfoundland fishermen.

Squanto's Patuxet family and villagers die from smallpox. He joins a village of Wampanoags under chief Massasoit.

Virginia in 1607. The Algonquian-speaking Powhatan chiefdom was ruled over by the paramount chief Wahunsonacock (also called Powhatan). Unlike the Iroquois confederation, the Powhatan chiefdom employed a hierarchical ruling structure with Wahunsonacock at the top, district chiefs and "priests" at the next level, war leaders at the third-highest rank, and commoners at the lowest level. Chiefs and other high-ranking leaders received tribute of foodstuffs, and controlled access to high-status items such as copper. Wahunsonacock's ability to rule rested with his religious power as demonstrated through his titles: Powhatan meant "one who dreams" while Mamanatowick has been interpreted as "my spirit, all the spirits," implying that his words and thoughts embodied great spiritual power. Powhatan women played important roles in politics, with some villages being ruled over by female relatives of Wahunsonacock and inheritance coming through the matrilineal line. As with the Iroquois and most eastern agricultural Indian peoples, Powhatan women did the planting and raising of crops of corn, squash, and beans, and gathered other foodstuffs such as berries. The men did the

Initially, the English at Jamestown sought trade and peace with the Powhatan Indians, and the Powhatans traded food for English-made items.

hunting, fishing, clearing of new fields for planting, and the fighting.

When Jamestown was established in 1607, the Powhatan population numbered around 15,000, spread over thirty villages. The chiefdom was then in the midst of expansion: Wahunsonacock had conquered the Kecoughtan tribe around 1597, wiped out the Chesapeakes around 1607, and then defeated the Piankatank tribe in 1608. The Powhatans attacked the

1620

December 21 English Separatists (Pilgrims) establish Plymouth Colony at the site of a Patuxet Indian village that had been wiped out by European diseases.

Squanto greets the Pilgrims by speaking English, much to their astonishment.

latter two tribes to forestall a prophecy of Powhatan priests that a nation arising in the east, along the Atlantic coast or along Chesapeake Bay, would bring an end to Wahunsonacock's empire. Such beliefs may have come from the actions of English survivors of the ill-fated Roanoke colony, who were believed to have lived among the Chesapeakes. The expansion of Wahunsonacock's empire, which originated along the James River near present-day Richmond, is also explained by the need to gain access to eastern areas and to maintain contact with Europeans and their trade items entering Chesapeake Bay.

When the English settled at Jamestown in 1607, they, like the Powhatans, intended to expand their presence in the Americas. The English hoped to discover instant wealth through gold or other valuable natural resources and to explore the Chesapeake Bay's many rivers in order to find a passage through the continent to Asia. They relied on Indians for food and quickly wore out their welcome. The

A romanticized portrayal of Pocahontas saving the life of John Smith in 1608.

1621

Wampanoag chief Massasoit and the Plymouth colonists, with Squanto as translator, establish a peace and collaborative agreement that lasts for five decades.

1622

March 22 Powhatans under Opechancanough revolt against the English in Virginia, killing more than 300 colonists. The Powhatans seek to restrict English settlement in the Jamestown area.

A label for Powhatan Brand Tobacco, demonstrating the importance of tobacco to colonial Virginia.

Powhatans scorned the hundred or so Englishmen who were incapable of feeding themselves, who had picked a swampy disease-ridden place at Jamestown Island to settle, who acted belligerently by forcibly taking corn from Indian villages, and who believed themselves culturally superior. In December 1607, the Powhatans captured Captain John Smith, interrogated him for two months, and metaphorically adopted him in an attempt to incorporate Jamestown as a district within the Powhatan chiefdom. Similarly, a few months later Captain Christopher Newport arrived on a supply ship from England with a "crown" to be placed on Wahunsonacock's head, making the Powhatan chief a vassal of King James. Ironically, both the English and the Powhatans viewed each other as subordinate peoples, setting up a scenario of conflicting goals. Hostility erupted throughout 1609 to 1614 as the English and Powhatans warred against each other. In 1610, known as the "starving time" in Jamestown history, the Powhatans blockaded Jamestown and nearly forced the English to abandon the colony. The conflict ended with the kidnapping of Pocahontas, one of Wahunsonacock's daughters, and her subsequent marriage to John Rolfe, a widower in Jamestown. There were approximately 500 to 600 Powhatan and English casualties.

From 1614 to 1622, peace reigned in the Virginia colony, but the seeds of a disastrous clash were being established. In those eight

A romanticized portrayal of Pocahontas as a princess, wearing stereotypical Plains Indian garb.

1622–1632

The war in Virginia lasts ten years, with the Powhatans greatly reduced in population and territory, but still sovereign at the end.

1623

English settlements are established at Dover and Portsmouth in New Hampshire, and at Casco Bay and Saco Bay in Maine.

1624

The Virginia Company loses its charter to the colony as a result of the 1622 attack, making Virginia a royal colony governed by a Crown-appointed governor.

years, several major new developments put the two peoples on a collision course. In 1614, the same man who had married Pocahontas developed a new tobacco strain, which gave the Virginia Company that ran the colony its first profitable venture. Because tobacco quickly exhausted the soil and more colonists tried to grow it in ever-increasing amounts, the English demand for Powhatan lands increased considerably. At the same time, the Virginia Company renewed and increased its efforts to convert Powhatans to Christianity; the English wanted to take children away from Indian families and raise them among English families in the colony. Powhatan parents viewed this initiative with skepticism and distrust. Wahunsonacock died in 1618 and his position was assumed by Opechancanough, who more militantly opposed English expansion and was the primary military leader of the Powhatans. The English killing of a popular Powhatan religious leader provided the spark for a massive

Bacon's Rebellion in Virginia in 1676 began as a war against Native Americans by small tobacco farmers on the Virginia frontier.

1626

New Netherlands governor Peter Minuit purchases Manhattan Island from the Shinnecock Indians.

1629-1633

The Zunis revolt and kill Spanish soldiers and missionaries in their village.

The Spanish in the Southwest force western pueblos of Acoma, Zuni, and Hopis to accept Catholic missionaries.

retaliation by the Powhatans on March 22, 1622. Approximately 350 English colonists were killed—over a quarter of the total English population in Virginia. Opechancanough had tried to teach the English a lesson; he warned Jamestown of the attack, and he attacked only outlying English settlements in order to force the English back to Jamestown. The war lasted ten years and ended in stalemate, but Powhatan numbers were greatly reduced by the war and diseases. One consequence of the attack for the English was that the Virginia Company lost its charter to the colony and the English Crown ruled the colony directly from 1624 onward.

Peace again reigned, but tensions increased over time. Between 1632 and 1644, the English continued to grab Powhatan land as immigration to Virginia increased and the colony became more dependent than ever on tobacco and, therefore, Indian land as a source of income. On April 18, 1644, the Powhatans, led by an aging Opechacanough, again attacked and killed more than 400 colonists in one day. The English captured Opechancanough and placed him in jail, where he was killed by an English soldier. This time the war lasted only two years and the

chiefdom was destroyed as a viable threat to the English. Remaining Powhatan peoples, such as the Pamunkeys, found themselves under attack in the early stages of Bacon's Rebellion in Virginia from 1675 to 1676. Indians from the North had attacked English farmers on the western frontier of Virginia, and the colonists now retaliated by assaulting whatever Indians they could find, including the remaining peace-loving Powhatans.

The English Invasion of New England

The permanent English settlement of New England began with the arrival of the Separatists, or Pilgrims, in 1620. They settled at the site of an abandoned Indian village called Patuxet, which the Pilgrims renamed Plymouth. Disease, probably plague, had struck the area from 1616 to 1618, killing nearly all the Patuxet people, and survivors had joined the neighboring Wampanoag Indians. Of the few survivors, one remarkable man greeted the Pilgrims in English. That man, named Squanto,

A painting portraying Squanto, who assisted the English Pilgrims in adjusting to a new land.

1630

October The Massachusetts Bay colony and Boston are established by Puritans.

1630–1639

The Great Migration of Puritans to New England, with around 20,000 arriving in the first decade.

1633

French trader Étienne Brûlé is killed by the Hurons.

Spanish Franciscans establish missions among the Apalachees.

Left: A romanticized portrait of a Pilgrim couple who settled in New England in the 1620s.

Right: An engraving of Wampanoag chief Samoset greeting the Pilgrims at Plymouth.

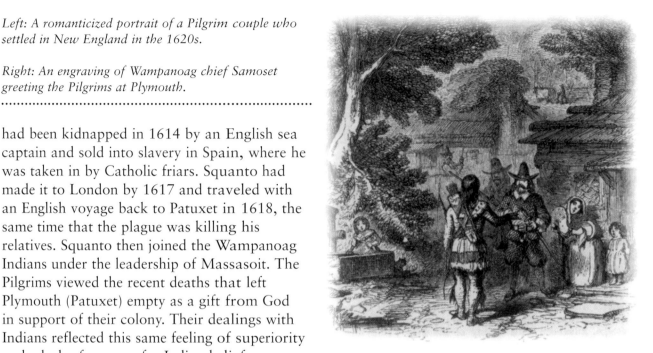

had been kidnapped in 1614 by an English sea captain and sold into slavery in Spain, where he was taken in by Catholic friars. Squanto had made it to London by 1617 and traveled with an English voyage back to Patuxet in 1618, the same time that the plague was killing his relatives. Squanto then joined the Wampanoag Indians under the leadership of Massasoit. The Pilgrims viewed the recent deaths that left Plymouth (Patuxet) empty as a gift from God in support of their colony. Their dealings with Indians reflected this same feeling of superiority and a lack of concern for Indian beliefs. Samoset, a Wampanoag chief, sealed a treaty of friendship with the Pilgrims, using Squanto as an interpreter, in 1621. The Wampanoag chiefs tried to use their alliance with the English to offset growing Narragansett Indian power in the region. This delicate balance became strained after 1630, when thousands of Puritans began to arrive in New England. The Puritans established the Massachusetts Bay colony and the Connecticut colony, and settlements such as Providence, Newport, and New Haven. The arrival of so many English people jeopardized relations with the Indians because of the Puritan demand for land and their lack of tolerance for

1633–1634

Smallpox ravages Indian populations throughout the Northeast and more than 10,000 Hurons die.

1634

March 25 Maryland is founded.

1635

The start of the "Beaver Wars" or "Mourning Wars" between the Iroquois and Hurons.

peoples unlike themselves. As one of New England's largest and most powerful Indian groups, the Pequots became caught in the middle between the Connecticut colony to the west and the Massachusetts Bay colony to the east. The Pequots also maintained trade relations with the Dutch in New Amsterdam, which angered the English. Additionally, the Narragansetts and Mohegans, with whom the Pequots had strained relations, lived on either side of them and allied themselves with the English to exert pressure on the Pequots. The Pequots controlled access to the whelk shells that were used to make wampum, which Indians used to construct memory belts for recording diplomatic meetings and other major events. The Puritans, realizing the high value placed on the shells by New England Indians, used them as money in trade with Indians, and sought greater access to the shells on Pequot land. The Pequots grew increasingly hostile to the Puritans because of these territorial pressures.

Pequot War

In 1633 and again in 1636, Indians killed a boatman on the waterways in New England,

This depiction of a battle in the Pequot War suggests the extreme brutality utilized by the Puritans and Pequot Indians.

1636–1637

The Pequot War occurs between Puritans and Pequots in New England. The Puritans are joined by Narragansett and Mohegan allies, and Pequot dominance in the region ends.

The Iroquois seek to eliminate Huron competition for European trade and to replenish their depleted population by forcibly adopting women and children from other Indian groups.

and the Puritans began to raise a justification for war. It was not known who had killed the first boatman, and Narragansetts had killed the second one, but the English used these acts of violence to go to war against the Pequots. The Pequot leader, Sassacus, failed in an attempt to persuade the Narragansetts to join them in the war against the English. Instead, the Narragansetts sided with the English and saw an opportunity to remove a rival tribe. Once hostilities began, the Pequots attacked outlying English settlements wherever they could and laid siege to Fort Saybrook in Connecticut. Both the Connecticut and Massachusetts Bay colonies formed armies to fight the Pequots. In the most dramatic action of the war, the English forces, together with their Mohegan and Narragansett allies, surrounded the stockaded main Pequot village, Fort Mystic, on June 1, 1637. Most Pequot warriors were out raiding English settlements, so the occupants of Fort Mystic were mostly women, children, and old men. The English set the fort and its buildings on fire and then shot or put to the sword all those who tried to escape. Pequot deaths have been estimated at around 600, while only two Puritan colonists died in the attack. Two months later, the English defeated the remaining Pequots. The Narragansett and Mohegan allies of the English expressed shock at the level of English brutality and mass killing. The Pequot chief, Sassacus, fled to Mohawk territory, where he was beheaded by them; they had little tolerance for the concerns of non-Iroquoian peoples and wanted to show the English that they were not involved in the war. Those remaining Pequots captured by the English were sold into slavery in Bermuda or divided up among the Mohegans and Narragansetts as captives in payment for their help. Pequot dominance in New England was over.

King Philip's War

The next serious conflict between the Puritans and Indians arose in King Philip's War from 1675 to 1676. The Wampanoags, led by a son of Massasoit named Metacom and known to the English as "King Philip," were under intense pressure from the English in the early 1670s to give up lands and to abide by English laws. The Wampanoags could not simply move westward because their enemies, the Iroquois, lived there

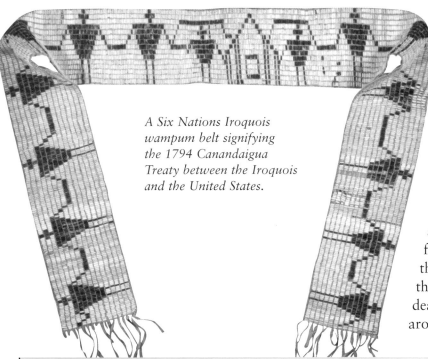

A Six Nations Iroquois wampum belt signifying the 1794 Canandaigua Treaty between the Iroquois and the United States.

1637

June 1 The Battle at Mystic River occurs, in which hundreds of Pequot men, women, and children die when their village is surrounded and set on fire by Puritan soldiers.

The Utes in the Great Basin area acquire Spanish horses through trade and raiding.

Narrangansett chief Miantonomi leads his warriors in support of the Puritans against the Pequots.

committed breaches of English laws were dragged into court and punished according to English custom, rather than being punished for such misdemeanors according to their own standards of behavior. Metacom had seen his father help the original English colonists in New England, but he grew up aware of the increasing injustice committed against his people by those same Englishmen and their descendants. After Massasoit died in 1661, Metacom and his brother Wamsutta tried to steer a middle course of cooperating with the English while also preserving their own autonomy. In 1662, however, Wamsutta died from an illness after being summoned to a Massachusetts Bay court to answer charges that he illegally sold lands to other colonies. Subsequently, the Puritans also grew wary of Metacom and distrusted his motivations. By 1671 the Puritans had perceived some plot against them on the part of Metacom and forced him and other Wampanoags to sign new treaties agreeing to pay taxes, give up their firearms, and relinquish land.

An illustration portraying an encounter during King Philip's War.

and opposed any such move, and the Wampanoags wanted to stay on the lands of their birth. The Wampanoags and other New England Indians had become increasingly dependent on English goods to survive. Many of them even lived in the English settlements to earn wages. Because they were living in close proximity to the English, Indians who

Animosity between the English and Wampanoags also grew because of intense missionary efforts on the part of the Puritans.

1640–1645

Kieft's War is waged between New Netherland (Willem Kieft was governor) and Indians on the lower Hudson River.

Lakota and Dakota (Sioux) groups separate from their relatives in the Minnesota area and begin to move westward onto the Great Plains.

1642

September The French found the settlement of Montreal.

In marked contrast to French Jesuits working further north and west, Puritan English missionaries insisted that before they could become Christians, New England Indians become "civilized" by cutting their hair, learning the English language, becoming literate, and dressing like the English. Indians, in other words, had to abandon their cultures entirely in order to become Christians. The Puritans, especially under the direction of Reverend John Eliot, insisted that potential Indian converts live with English families or in English-dominated "praying towns." Beginning in 1646, Eliot established fourteen praying towns. He learned the Massachusett language and translated the Old and New Testaments of the Bible with the help of dozens of converted Indians. The fourteen praying towns had 2,500 Indian students by 1675. Christianized Indians played a role in the start of King Philip's War when English courts convicted and executed three Wampanoag men for the murder of a

....

Reverend John Eliot preaching to New England Algonquian Indians, many of whom he converted and set up in "praying towns."

1642–1643

Susquehannock Indians and Maryland colonists are at war. Susquehannocks are aided by the New Sweden colony on Delaware Bay.

1643

February 25 In an incident called "Kieft's Massacre," Dutch soldiers kill 120 Algonquian men, women, and children at the site of today's Jersey City.

Providence colony founder Roger Williams publishes *Key to the Indian Languages.*

Christianized Indian named John Sassamon, who had warned the English that King Philip was organizing an attack on them. This was the first time that the Puritan courts had prosecuted an Indian person for an Indian crime, and many Wampanoags and other New England Indians took exception to the precedent it established.

Within days of the hanging of the three convicted Wampanoag men, attacks followed in revenge. An Englishman killed a Wampanoag man attacking his cattle, and Indian assaults on English settlements from the Atlantic Ocean to the Connecticut River began. The Nipmucs and Narragansetts soon joined the Wampanoags as they inflicted heavy losses on the English. The Puritans repeated their atrocities of the Pequot War by massacring hundreds of Narragansett men, women, and children, as well as Englishmen with Indian spouses—an incident known as the Great Swamp Fight of December 1675. Metacom and some of his followers traveled to the Dutch colony's capital at Albany, seeking to regroup and enlist the support of the Iroquois, but the Iroquois attacked them and drove them back to New England. The colonies of Massachusetts, Plymouth, Rhode Island, and

Wampanoag leader Metacom, known to the Puritans in New England as "King Philip."

Connecticut all launched armies against the Wampanoags and other New England Indians fighting against the English. Some Indians helped the English: the Mohegans, the few remaining Pequots, and others who sought to preserve their autonomy by siding with what they perceived to be the dominant power in the region. The English enjoyed superior numbers and firepower, and eventually they harried the Indian forces to the point that Metacom and his followers lacked food, ammunition, and other basic supplies. The English eventually killed Metacom in a swamp in August 1676, and the English commander at the scene ordered for his body to be decapitated and dismembered; the head was displayed on a pole in Plymouth for years. Metacom's wife and one of his sons were sold into slavery in the West Indies

1644

April 18 Powhatans under Opechancanough again attack English settlers in Virginia, killing more than 500 colonists.

Opechancanough is captured and killed in captivity, and the war dies down quickly, forever ending Powhatan dominance in eastern Virginia.

A Pueblo spiritual leader; men like him led the Pueblo Revolt of 1680 against the Spanish in New Mexico.

along with other Wampanoag, Nipmuc, and Narragansett survivors. King Philip's War resulted in 600 English dead, 1,200 houses burned, and 8,000 head of cattle killed, while more than 3,000 Indians died and hundreds more were sold into slavery. The Wampanoags, Nipmucs, and Narragansetts were virtually exterminated in this war, and Indian resistance in southern New England ebbed.

Spanish-Indian Relations in the Southwest

After Juan de Oñate led the colonization of northern Mexico (New Mexico) at the end of the sixteenth century, more Spanish settlers and missionaries moved into the area in the succeeding decades. In 1610 the capital of Spanish New Mexico was constructed at Santa Fe, and Indian laborers built most of the city. Catholic Franciscan missionaries also came, and the emphasis on Indian conversion increased throughout the seventeenth century. Well-connected Spanish settlers received grants of land and the support of the colonial government to co-opt Indian labor to run ranches and farms, and the colonial government insisted on tributes of food from Indian villages. Over time,

individual Indian pueblos rebelled against the demands placed on them by the Spanish, while the Spanish responded with harsh punishments and military intervention.

Pueblo Revolt

Tensions between the pueblos and the Spanish increased over time. The Franciscans banned many religious practices, such as dancing, and raided the underground kivas where Pueblo Indians conducted religious rituals and held meetings. More fundamentally, the priests taught that sex, especially between unmarried couples, was a sin that brought eternal damnation, whereas Pueblo Indians regarded sex as a life-affirming and perhaps sacred act. The patriarchal nature of the Catholic Church threatened the traditional power of Pueblo women over agricultural produce, families, and their own fertility. Although some Pueblo people expressed an interest in the new Catholic religion, missionaries were unable to supplant the Pueblo religion, as it literally went underground into the kivas. In addition to cultural pressures placed on them by the Spanish, the pueblos also suffered through a loss of population

1646–1675

Puritan minister John Eliot establishes "praying towns" among New England Indians, especially at Natick.

Eliot teaches Native people English and has them translate the Bible and other Puritan religious tracts into Native languages to aid in converting all Indian people in the region to Christianity.

A Pueblo religious ceremony; Spanish officials tried to outlaw Pueblo religion in the seventeenth century.

in the seventeenth century due to European diseases. The population in 1581 numbered about 130,000 in sixty-one pueblos. By 1600 the population had dropped to about 60,000. By 1638 it was down to 40,000. And by 1680 there were only 17,000 Pueblo Indians living in forty-six pueblos.

In the 1670s, a prolonged drought struck the Southwest, leaving Pueblo Indians hungry while the Spanish colonists demanded greater amounts of food tribute. Attacks from neighboring Navajo and Apache Indians increased, and the Spanish were unable to protect the pueblos, further threatening their security. In response, Pueblo Indians initiated what scholars call a spiritual revitalization movement whereby they returned to their traditional religion with vehemence in order to try to restore the spiritual and ecological balance that traditionally characterized their lives in the Southwest. The Franciscans repressed this return to traditional religion by arresting forty-seven Pueblo spiritual healers in 1675. The Spanish executed three of

1647

In northern Florida, Spanish missionaries try to interfere with Apalachee traditional culture and chiefly succession.

Apalachees revolt against Spanish missions, burning seven of eight missions to the ground and killing three priests.

1648–1657

Iroquois expand their war against the Hurons to other Native peoples in the Northeast and Great Lakes areas.

the healers for practicing witchcraft, and a fourth died in Spanish custody. The other healers were whipped publicly and imprisoned, but were released after Pueblo chiefs demanded an end to the punishment.

One of the Pueblo healers who had been whipped and then released was a man named Popé from the San Juan pueblo. While taking refuge at the Taos pueblo in northern New Mexico, he planned a massive uprising by all of the pueblos, to occur on the same day. Other Pueblo leaders played important organizational roles in the revolt that took place in August 1680, but the religious dimension was the unifying force. When the Pueblo Indians rebelled, they destroyed Catholic churches and symbols in their villages. Pueblo religious leaders "unbaptized" Indian converts, bathing them in local rivers to wash away the stain of Christianity. The Pueblo Indians also killed twenty-one priests and missionaries, and about 380 other Spaniards. The Spanish retreated to Santa Fe, where the Pueblo Indians besieged them for nine days and cut off the water supply. Governor Don Antonio de Otermín led the Spanish forces that fought through the blockade

A Piegan man holding a medicine pipe, or peace pipe. Shamans were sought after for their medical knowledge.

and retreated all the way back to Mexico City. The Spanish did not return until 1692, and the Pueblo Revolt remains one of the most successful American Indian rebellions against Europeans. When the Spanish came back to New Mexico, they had learned some lessons regarding how much they could control Indians by force; never again did they try so directly to impose their religion and culture with brute force. Beginning in the 1690s, Pueblo Indians and Spaniards worked to establish a cultural compromise and created a society that was part Indian and part Spanish.

Spanish-Indian Relations in Florida

By 1602 there were 1,200 Christian Indians living around St. Augustine. Spain decided that military conquest of Indians was too expensive, compared with relying on gifts to chiefs who led people into accepting missionaries. Spain established a string of dozens of missions across northern Florida among the Timucuas and Apalachees. The Timucuas proved most amenable to the mission system and, by 1608, Spanish officials had brought about peace between the Timucuas and Apalachees to their

1649

The Iroquois, armed with Dutch guns, destroy Huron villages and kill, adopt, or disperse the Huron population.

Establishment of the Company for the Propagation of the Gospel in New England, which conducted missionary work among Indians.

1656

Timucuas revolt against Spanish missions in Florida for making their chiefs perform manual labor like the commoners. They kill all the Spanish soldiers and civilians at the San Pedro mission.

An eighteenth-century view of St. Augustine, Florida, which was established by the Spanish in 1565 and used as a base of operations to build a string of Catholic missions.

1660

Mohawk woman Kateri Tekakwitha survives a smallpox epidemic that kills her family, and converts to Catholicism.

1661

Massasoit, leader of the Wampanoags in Massachusetts, dies, leaving his two sons, Metacom and Wamsutta, in power.

west. Missionaries began to live among the Apalachees in 1633. Less than two decades later, in 1647, the Apalachees revolted against the mission system and destroyed seven of the eight missions in their villages, executing three missionaries. After a decade of missionary activity, Apalachee villages had divided between traditionalists and Christian converts. Spanish missionaries and officials favored the converts and extended more goods and favors to them. The converts receiving the favors asserted their own right to rule in the villages, directly threatening the power and privilege of chiefs who inherited their positions and maintained them by traditional means. After pitched battles between Apalachee traditionalists and the Spanish with their Indian allies, the Spanish won and put down the rebellion. In 1656 the Timucuas revolted against Spanish rule. Distinctively, the Timucuas deliberately spared the priests, as many Timucua leaders had become Catholic and literate. The Spanish had tried to make chiefs perform manual labor in

Engraving of Frenchman Jacque Le Moyne's 1564 print of French soldiers aiding Florida Indians in battle.

1662

Wamsutta's brother Metacom ("King Philip") blames the English for Wamsutta's death and begins to plan an uprising.

Wampanoag leader Wamsutta dies after a peace council with the governor of Massachusetts.

1668

The British form the Hudson's Bay Company, and trade guns and other items to Indian people.

opposition to their traditional privileges as elites. The Timucua revolt lasted just six months and was ended by Spanish cavalry and Apalachee allies. In the aftermath of the Indian revolts, the Spanish in Florida realized that the best way to govern these societies was to leave the traditional power structure intact and to work through the established chiefs.

The Spanish presence in the seventeenth-century Southeast produced other impacts on Indians in the region, which dramatically altered Indian cultures and populations. The principal changes occurred in Native religions. The Timucuas and Apalachees abandoned the use of burial and temple mounds, opting instead for Christian-style burials and Catholic chapels. Indian social organization and material culture remained little changed. Spanish policy forbade guns being traded to Indians, but some Spanish firearms were traded nonetheless and have been found in archaeological remains among groups well into the southern interior. Cultural

Charles Town (Charleston), South Carolina, the center of the English slave trade for southeastern Indians.

1670

Indians armed with English guns attack other Indians who do not possess the weapons, causing them to flee to other parts of the Southeast.

The English establish Carolina colony at Charles Town.

The English in Carolina develop an economy based on acquiring deerskins and Indian slaves from their Indian allies.

A hackneyed portrayal of Spanish brutality and their enslavement of Indian people. All European colonial powers enslaved Indians for profit and labor.

adaptation was a two-way street. The Spanish, for example, used Indian-made pottery. Not only were Christianity and literacy introduced in Indian communities in Florida, but deadly diseases were too; the Timucuas experienced four epidemics of smallpox between 1613 and 1672, and epidemics struck periodically well into the eighteenth century. The greatest epidemic to hit the Spanish missions in Florida—and to the Apalachee and Timucua Indians—came from the North in the late seventeenth century and early eighteenth century.

English-Indian Relations in South Carolina

When English sugar plantation owners from Barbados and Jamaica began to move to the new colony of Carolina in present-day South Carolina, they sought Indian slaves. Charles Town (as Charleston was called until the American Revolution) was founded by Caribbean plantation owners in 1670. Its first four to five decades of prosperity was based on the deerskin trade with Indians, and on seizing Indians and either selling them as slaves to the Caribbean or using them as slaves on Carolina plantations. The English encouraged Indian

1675

January The death of a Christianized Indian named Samoset provides the immediate spark for King Philip's War. Samoset had warned the English that Metacom was planning an attack and was then found murdered or drowned in an icy pond.

1675–1676

King Philip's War is fought in New England between Puritans and an Indian confederation of Wampanoags, Nipmucks, Mohegans, Narragansetts, and Podunks.

Nominally led by Metacom, the Indians attack fifty-two of the ninety English towns in New England, killing hundreds of colonists and thousands of English cattle.

Left: A stereotyped image of one Indian scalping another, serving as proof of an Indian's exploits.

Right: Throughout the continent, Indians displayed scalps in order to demonstrate their prowess as warriors.

tribes to turn on one another and go to war in order to take captives and then sell them to the English. In return, Indian slave traders received all sorts of trade goods, including guns, ammunition, manufactured cloth, and metal items such as knives, needles, hatchets, and hoes. It was at this time, after 1670, that southeastern Indians gained an economic incentive to capture Indians from other tribes and sell them to Europeans as slaves.

The Carolinians looked southward to the Spanish territory in present-day northern Florida and southeastern Georgia for a source of Indian slaves. The English in Carolina found themselves only 250 miles from Spanish-controlled St. Augustine, whereas they were a full 500 miles from Chesapeake Bay, where the nearest English settlement was located. Conflict between the English in Carolina and the Spanish, as well as between their respective Indian allies, was nearly inevitable as the Spanish sought to remove English intrusion into their lands, and the English felt they had the right of occupation as granted by their king. Because the English in

1676

Bacon's Rebellion occurs in Virginia. Tobacco farmers rebel against their government's inability to protect them from Indian attacks.

Led by Nathaniel Bacon, a wealthy cousin of the Virginia governor, farmers attack friendly Powhatan and Susquehannock Indians in the colony.

August 12 The English in New England kill Metacom in a swamp, then sell his wife, son, and 500 other Wampanoags into slavery in the West Indies.

Carolina were initially dependent on the deerskin trade and Indian slavery for profits, they provided guns to Indians living near Charles Town and encouraged them to attack other Indians, especially those allied with the Spanish and living in Catholic mission towns along the Atlantic coast and across northern Florida.

Indian and English Slavery

Before Europeans arrived in the Americas, and for hundreds of years afterward, American Indians in the Southeast and elsewhere seized captives when they went to war. If the captives were adult men, and

....

Tomochichi (1644–1739) was chief of the Yamacraw Creeks located on the Savannah River.

therefore enemy warriors, they were likely to be ritually tortured and killed in the villages of their captors. If the captives were children or women, they were much more likely to be adopted by their captors. The fate of captives was not based on economic necessity but on social reasons.

The torture of adult male captives enabled Indians to fulfill a sacred obligation to avenge the deaths of kin. Adoption, on the other hand, enabled a family to replace members who had died, and adopted war captives enjoyed all the privileges extended to relatives by birth. Some Indian groups, like the Iroquois in New York, waged war against other Indians after European contact specifically to acquire new kinsmen to replace those who had died from disease or in war. A few captives underwent neither torture nor adoption but remained on the

fringe of their new society. Europeans called this anomalous status "slavery" among Indians, because they often performed strenuous work. Nevertheless, the goals of Indians seizing captives did not include economic enrichment.

Until 1680 the cornerstone of Carolina Indian policy was an alliance with the neighboring Westo Indians, refugees from the Lake Erie area pushed out by the Iroquois wars. As early as 1675, rumors reached the Spanish in the Timucua and Apalachee missions in northern Florida that the English were training their Indian allies, such as the Westos, to attack the missions. From 1680 English-sponsored Westo raids were made on the Guale missions along today's Georgia coast. The main goals for the English were to acquire Indian slaves and reduce Spanish power in the region. In a few short years, the Guale missions were destroyed, with hundreds of mission Indians either captured and sold to the English, or killed. The enslaved Guale Indians were then sold by the Carolinians to the West Indies to work on sugar plantations.

In 1680 a war broke out between the Westos and Shawnees. This war involved Carolinians on both sides and was a battle over the future direction of Indian affairs in the young English

1680

The Pueblo Revolt in the Southwest succeeds in driving the Spanish out of New Mexico for twelve years.

Led by the spiritual leader Popé from the Taos pueblo, the Pueblo Revolt is a well-planned assault on Spanish missionaries and soldiers by nearly every pueblo in New Mexico.

colony. The Westos were supplied by Carolina proprietors, or planters, and the Shawnees by Carolina deerskin traders. The Shawnees won and remaining Westos assimilated into other groups. The Shawnees took the place of the Westos as the group that was supplied with guns and encouraged to attack other Indians for skins and slaves. In addition, because of the Shawnee victory, the deerskin traders in Carolina controlled the direction of Indian affairs in the colony for several more decades, therefore guaranteeing that the pursuit of Indian slaves would continue unabated.

Over the next two decades, the English made alliances with other Native groups such as the Yamassees, Cherokees, Creeks, and Chickasaws. The English traded guns to them and then encouraged them to attack other Indian peoples in order to acquire captives, and to hunt deer in order to trade deerskins. It was at this time that Indian allies of the English, who were well-armed with guns, began to attack the Choctaws and the smaller Gulf Indian groups that did not

The seizure and selling of Indian slaves, along with the deerskin trade, built the first fortunes in Carolina.

The English and Savannah Indians in South Carolina wage war on the Westo Indians. The Westos are eliminated as trade middlemen between the Carolinians and other Indians.

The English in Carolina initiate a lucrative slave trade in Indian captives, who are captured by Native allies of the English and then sold to English slavers.

c. 1680–1750

Lakota Sioux continue their move from the eastern woodlands to the plains.

Plains Indians acquire horses, making buffalo hunting easier.

yet possess firearms. Such attacks remained sporadic, however, until the turn of the century and the eruption of another European war that produced significant impacts in the South.

The War of the Spanish Succession in North America lasted from 1701 to 1713, and pitted England against France and Spain. The Carolinians organized attacks against both France and Spain and their Native allies during the war. The Spanish still claimed what is now Florida and maintained a string of mission outposts among their Indian allies, such as the Timucuas and Apalachees across northern Florida. The French had established a presence on the Gulf of Mexico in 1699, and realized that they must depend on Indian allies along the Gulf Coast and in the interior lower Mississippi valley. French power rested on alliances with Indians and especially the Choctaws, who were considered the key to the country because of their large population (between 15,000 and 20,000), and their hatred of the English for encouraging slave-raiding attacks on their towns.

During the War of the Spanish Succession,

A fur trader plying his Native customer with alcohol, a common tactic used by Euro-Americans to cheat Indians.

1681

March 4 Pennsylvania is established as a British colony.

1682–1683

June 23 The treaty of friendship is signed between the Lenape (Delawares) and William Penn of the Pennsylvania colony.

1683

The Spanish close their Guale missions.

the Carolinians first turned their attention to the Spanish mission towns in northern Florida. Carolinians under Governor James Moore led attacks by the Shawnees, Yamassees, and Lower Creeks against the Spanish missions among the Apalachee Indians. The most devastating of these English-sponsored attacks came in 1704 and 1705. Despite attempts by Apalachees and missionaries to resist, they were quickly defeated, mission towns were sacked, and hundreds of captives were marched to Charles Town for sale to the Caribbean. In 1706 the missions among the Timucua Indians also fell to English and Indian attacks. An English and Indian force led by trader Thomas Nairne even raided southward all the way to the Florida Keys. The English sent more than a thousand mission Indian captives to Barbados as slaves, and an unknown number to other North American English colonies such as Virginia, Pennsylvania, New York, and New England. Ostensibly, the Carolinians acted to protect their colony from European competitors and enemies by

Castillo de San Marcos, constructed by the Spanish in the seventeenth century to protect St. Augustine from attack.

1684

Indians destroy an attempted colony at Galveston Bay by René-Robert Cavelier, Sieur de La Salle.

The Yamasees raid the Timucua mission of Santa Catalina de Afuyca.

The French build Lake Nipigon Post in Assiniboine country, Canada.

Yamasee chief Altamaha leads the Yamasees to the mouth of the Savannah River near Stuarts Town.

A Creek, or Seminole, Indian man from the nineteenth century. Seminoles were Creeks who moved into Florida.

obliterating the Native allies of Spain and France, but their desire for profit in acquiring Indian slaves shaped their actions more than geopolitical concerns. However, the Spanish presence in the South was restricted to the St. Augustine and Pensacola areas after these attacks on the mission towns in the first few years of the eighteenth century. Britain and France now provided the principal European rivalry in the South.

We will never know the exact number of slaves seized by English traders and their Indian allies in the lower Mississippi River valley. Before 1700, the Chickasaws in present-day northern Mississippi, and the Creeks in present-day Georgia and Alabama, formed a trading alliance with the Carolinians, acquired firearms, and began raiding their neighbors, such as the Choctaws, to seize captives for sale as slaves to the English. Anecdotally, we know these raids caused devastation to Indians who did not enjoy an alliance with England. When French officials first met Choctaw representatives in 1702, they were told that the Choctaws had

Apalachee Indian iconography. Apalachees were nearly exterminated by their Native and English neighbors.

already lost 500 villagers to Chickasaw slave raiders, with another 1,800 killed. During the War of the Spanish Succession, at least three large British-sponsored expeditions declared war on the Choctaws and sought slaves. In 1706 a raid carried off 300 women and

1686

Frenchmen under Henri de Tonti establish a trading post at the mouth of the Arkansas River along the Mississippi River.

1689–1697

King William's War draws in eastern Indians on the side of either England or France as the European conflict spills over into North America.

Plains Indians waging war on horseback; horses vastly changed Native lifestyles throughout North America.

children; another attack in 1708 captured an unknown yet significant number of Choctaws; and a third force comprising an army of Chickasaws and an army of Creeks took 330 captives in 1711. Altogether, Britain obtained at least 2,500 captives from the Choctaws by 1712, and an unknown number of Indians were killed in the attacks. The bitter feelings of revenge caused by the Chickasaw slave raids persisted until the late 1750s, as the Choctaws and Chickasaws remained at war for the entire period. Smaller Indian groups along the Gulf Coast and the Mississippi River also suffered periodic attacks, losing dozens of people at once. Slave-raiding attacks, combined with exposure to deadly diseases, reduced the populations of groups like the Taensas and Tunicas to almost zero in the early 1700s. The Carolinians had the option of trading with Indian groups such as the Choctaws, and securing them as allies to counter French inroads in the lower Mississippi valley, but the desire for profit overrode other diplomatic choices. Profit and trade, along with incessant warfare, dominated Indian-European relations in the eighteenth century.

1692

Pequot chief Robin Cassasinamon dies.

The Spanish return to New Mexico and reestablish Santa Fe as the colony's capital.

1699

French settlers under Jean-Baptiste Le Moyne establish Biloxi and French presence in the lower Mississippi valley.

The French establish the Cahokia trading post in the lower Missouri River region.

1700–1800

Beaver pelts—trapped in Canada, the Northeast, and the Great Lakes area—brought profits to Indian and European fur traders, and warmth and fashion to Europeans. South of the Ohio River, Indians traded deerskins to colonists for sale in Europe.

Europeans traveled to Indian villages to obtain furs and created companies to manage the immense fur trade that became crucial to the colonial economies of the late seventeenth and eighteenth centuries. Indian people adapted easily to the new demand for animals that they already hunted on a limited scale, and the trade enabled them to acquire a wide range of European-made merchandise.

Left: Euro-American fur traders and American Indians camping. The fur trade provided a principal avenue of inter-cultural cooperation.
Right: American Indians carrying beaver furs destined for trade with Europeans.

Beavers and deer provided the main impetus for the fur trade, but Europeans sought furs from other animals too, such as martens, rabbits, bears, mountain lions, fox, and buffalo. Europeans extracted two products from beavers. The soft underbelly fur provided effective insulation against the cold and was ideal for making felt, used to manufacture hats and winter coats in Europe. The castoreum, a yellow sticky oil excreted by beavers during mating, became a base for perfumes made in Europe, especially France. Deerskins were also used in leatherworking (one of the largest industries in eighteenth-century London), to make book bindings, clothing (particularly working-class men's trousers and aprons), gloves, footwear, and in the

North American colonies, a floppy wide-brimmed hat called the "South Carolina hat," and horse harnesses and saddles. Indeed, beaver furs and deerskins were so valuable by the late seventeenth century that they served as currency in the colonies to buy almost any sort of merchandise. The American slang for a dollar—a buck—may date from this era, as buckskins provided the standard of measurement for buying manufactured items in the southern colonies.

Although every European country that established a colony in North America engaged in the fur trade to one degree or another (the fur trade was the major motivating factor behind Russian colonization of the northwestern coast, starting in the 1740s), it was the French and British who had the greatest impact. French *coureurs des bois* (runners of the woods) traveled deep into Indian country and engaged in the fur trade without licenses from the French government throughout the seventeenth century. French *voyageurs* participated legally in the fur trade with licenses granted by French officials. Both groups of Frenchmen extended the reach of France deep into the North American interior

and played instrumental roles in maintaining good relations between Indian groups and the French colonial governments. Founded in 1670, the Hudson's Bay Company brought British fur traders into the far north of Canada to compete with French voyageurs. The Hudson's Bay Company expanded dramatically throughout the eighteenth century, extending the reach of European fur traders throughout the 1.5-million-square-mile drainage basin of Hudson's Bay all the way into the northern plains and Rocky Mountains. The Hudson's Bay Company constructed a string of forts, or trading posts, throughout the region under their jurisdiction, where Indians brought furs to be traded and where European governance of these areas originated. In 1779 the British established another major fur trading company at Montreal, the North West Company, which competed with the Hudson's Bay Company and pushed the fur trade enterprise all the way to the Pacific Ocean. In 1821 the two competitors merged into one company.

....

A French-Canadian fur trapper. Trappers built extensive trade networks with Native clients.

1700

Chickasaws armed with English guns attack Caddos west of the Mississippi River.

Cheyennes enter the plains.

January 26 A massive earthquake and tsunami strike the northwestern coast.

1701

August 4 The Iroquois pledge to stay out of future European conflicts and establish peace with both France and Britain. French officials refer to this diplomatic initiative as the "Great Peace of Montreal."

The Society for the Propagation of the Gospel in Foreign Parts is founded by Britain to conduct missionary work among Indians in North America.

Numbers of beaver furs exported out of North America are hard to gauge, but the animal quickly became depleted in northeastern North America, forcing traders to travel farther afield in search of Indian people who still had access to beaver. It is estimated that several million white-tailed deer lived in the South when Europeans arrived. From 1699 to 1715, South Carolina exported an average of 54,000 deerskins a year out of Charles Town, and thereafter the trade only increased, reaching 150,000 skins shipped to London from South Carolina during the mid-eighteenth century. The British, Spanish, and French also exported thousands of deerskins annually from New Orleans, Savannah, Mobile, Pensacola, and St. Augustine, reaching a total of nearly 500,000 per year by the middle of the eighteenth century.

The Impact of the Fur Trade on Indian People

Indian people had always trapped beaver for fur and hunted deer for food. Deer provided as much as a third of the annual diet for most Indians in the Southeast, and they used the various parts of the animal carcass to make tools, clothing, and ritual objects. Beaver

Map of Hudson's Bay at the time of the Seven Years' War, showing French and British trading posts, including Fort York, the principal trading post of the Hudson's Bay Company.

1701–1713

The War of the Spanish Succession in North America draws in eastern Indians on the side of either England or France and Spain as the European conflict spills over into North America.

1702

The French establish Mobile, in present-day Alabama.

1703–1704

English and Indian allies from Carolina destroy Spanish mission towns in northern Florida and enslave the Indian survivors.

trapping and deer hunting for the European trade was, on one hand, merely an extension of Native practices. On the other hand, they had never before killed so many animals at once. This slaughter of beaver and deer rivaled the killing of buffalo on the Great Plains two centuries later and reached crisis proportions by the mid- to late-eighteenth century when beaver and deer numbers diminished.

Obtaining European Goods

The main driving force behind Indian willingness to overhunt certain animals and participate in the European trade was to obtain European goods. Indians wanted such manufactured items as woven cloth, blankets, clothing, shoes, guns, ammunition, paint, hatchets, knives, brass kettles, and other brass and copper items such as metal hoes, bells, scissors, buttons, combs, and sewing needles. These European-made goods replaced Indian-made items with more durable versions (metal knives had sharper edges and lasted longer than

A stereotypical portrayal of Indians hunting near present-day San Francisco with bow and arrows.

1706

The Comanches migrate eastward from the Rocky Mountains to the plains.

1709

French Jesuit Joseph Aubrey begins working at the St. Francis mission among the Abenakis.

1710

June 8 The Treaty of Conestoga is signed between Pennsylvania and the Iroquois. The Iroquois offer themselves as mediators between the Pennsylvania colony and Indians residing in the colony.

September Swiss and German colonists establish the town of New Bern, North Carolina.

stone, wood, or bone knives, for example), or they offered greater abundance of high-status materials, such as copper. Indian individuals or tribes in a given area could sometimes control access to Europeans, forcing other Indians to trade through them and enriching themselves in the process. Economic motivations to acquire European trade items often became secondary, however, to the chance of gaining higher status and demonstrating an ability to interact successfully with powerful foreigners by acquiring their products. Chiefs or other local leaders could use their ability to access manufactured goods to distribute gifts to their relatives and supporters, thereby ensuring their high status through reciprocal obligations. Indian groups who obtained guns before

A Nootka Indian gull mask from Vancouver Island, off the Northwest coast.

their neighbors frequently used the weapons to wage war on them, making access to the trade in firearms an imperative for all Native peoples in North America.

One trade item that severely disrupted Indian communities was alcohol. All European colonial powers traded furs for alcohol at one time or another, but the British relied heavily on rum as a trade item because of the immense profit that could be had from trading watered-down kegs of rum for beaver furs or deerskins. In the eighteenth century, Indians throughout eastern North America complained about the negative effects of

alcohol on their villages. Drunken Indians, especially young men, assaulted each other and other villagers, neglected their duties to provide for their families, and sometimes caused increased tensions between different peoples by attacking Europeans or Indians from another tribe. Both Indian leaders and colonial officials from all European nations called for stricter trade regulations to prevent such disruptions, but independent fur traders circumvented the law in search of profit. In addition, some Indian people engaged in trade out of self-serving motivations in an attempt to build up status within their society. At times, independent action sparked conflict, such as when the Choctaw warrior Red Shoes opened trade with the South Carolinians in the 1740s even though most Choctaws traded with the French based in New Orleans. A civil war among the Choctaws erupted over the issue, which lasted for several years and resulted in hundreds of deaths. One strategy employed by many Indian groups to control the fur trade and limit its negative aspects was

1711–1713

The Tuscarora War occurs between Carolina settlers and Tuscarora Indians in North Carolina. The Tuscaroras and other Indian peoples from eastern North Carolina react against the spread of European settlements in the area.

1712–1750

Mesquakie (Fox) wars against France and its Native allies.

1713

The French establish the Natchitoches trading post.

to invite European traders to marry into their families. In the eighteenth century, this became a popular strategy among many Indian groups in the South. As British trade came to dominate after the end of the Seven Years' War between Britain and France in 1763, entrepreneurial British traders flooded the Southeast and used alcohol as their primary trade item. Numerous elite Indian families among the Cherokees, Creeks, Choctaws, and Chickasaws tried to limit the destructiveness of this trade by marrying their daughters and nieces to Euro-American fur traders. This intermarriage enabled certain Indian families to maintain access to and control over European goods, and it helped to prevent abuses such as cheating on payments, assaulting women, and trading alcohol. By intermarrying with Euro-American traders, these Indian groups also produced children who remained Indian (matrilineal societies and children belonged to the family of their mother) while also gaining the knowledge and language skills of both their Indian and

American Indians trading furs to Europeans in exchange for manufactured goods.

Euro-American relations. Such bicultural offspring sometimes went on to play key roles in European-Indian relations as traders, interpreters, and diplomats, and a few later became tribal leaders in their own right.

In the eighteenth century, Indian peoples in

eastern North America grew dependent on European manufactured goods. They no longer made certain items and instead turned to trading to get basic supplies and tools. They had no choice but to rely on Europeans for guns, gunpowder, and ammunition. Such dependence

1714–1715

Chipewyan people who live along the Churchill River in Canada are attacked by Crees from northeastern Canada armed with European firearms.

1715

April The Yamassees are in deep debt to Carolina traders and no longer have access to abundant deer herds or potential Indian captives after years of the fur trade and Indian slave trade have depleted resources.

Carolina traders seize Yamassee women and children, and the Yamassees respond with a massive rebellion. The Yamassee War is fought between the English and the Yamassees.

Surviving Yamassees join other Native groups in the Southeast, such as the Creeks.

often led to debt, which caused friction between Indians and Europeans throughout the century as beaver and deer numbers decreased and the ability of Indians to pay off debts decreased along with them. The fur trade also introduced the profit motive among Indians, and some adapted to the world of European-manufactured items and increasing debt by seeking other ways of making money to buy the goods they wanted. The impact of Indian participation in the market economy, the owning of African-American slaves, and the introduction of the concept of private property is seen most dramatically in the nineteenth century, but it was the fur trade that began this transformation of Indian cultures, politics, and economies.

A World at War

Although violent conflicts of Indians against Europeans, and Indian groups against one another, had existed since the times of first contact, warfare of both types increased significantly in the eighteenth century. As

An image from the eighteenth century showing French trade with Indians of the lower Mississippi Valley.

1718

August 12 The French establish New Orleans.

1719

September 27 Frenchman Bénard La Harpe visits Wichita villages and establishes trade relations.

1721

The Spanish establish Los Adaes in Texas.

Timucua Indians showing Florida Indians preparing for war by consulting a shaman.

Europeans established new colonial settlements, increased their trade with Indians, and engaged in war with one another, Indian people were forced to handle new pressures and crises. From the late 1600s, a time of endemic warfare was common due to the increasingly intrusive European presence. The eighteenth century can be characterized as a time of war periodically broken up by short-lived truces.

A constant state of war was not necessarily a natural state of affairs among Indian communities. Unlike professional European soldiers, Indian warriors were also fathers, sons, and brothers who were still expected to provide for their families by hunting and trading. American Indian war parties stayed in the field temporarily until the specific task they had agreed to participate in was accomplished or until a bad omen presented itself and caused a need to regroup. Indian soldiers required that rituals to empower their war medicine be performed before they went to war, or else they risked defeat by not gaining spiritual sanction. Similarly, when a war party returned to the villages, certain rituals had to be carried out to ensure that feelings of vengeance and aggression

1722

January New England colonists raid the Abenaki mission town of Norridgewock.

The Tuscaroras formally become the sixth nation of the Iroquois Confederacy.

1722–1727

Anglo-Abenaki wars are fought in northern New England.

1729–1730

November 28 Natchez Indians revolt against the French. Hundreds of African slaves join the Natchez Indians. France responds by urging the Choctaws to attack the Natchez.

The Natchez disperse throughout the Southeast, with some Natchez joining the Chickasaws, others joining the Creeks, and others joining the Cherokees.

British General John Burgoyne urging Indians to attack the American rebels during the American Revolution.

were left outside the community. Europeans, on the other hand, with the exception of local colonial militia units, used professional armies that stayed out in the field doing battle as long as was deemed necessary. They did not have to feed families, and war could therefore be a full-time occupation.

After Europeans arrived to stay in North America at the beginning of the seventeenth century, Indians fought wars against other Indians—at the instigation of European allies, or for more traditional reasons of revenge, or for reasons of trade, such as the Iroquois "Mourning Wars" of the 1640s. In siding with a European ally in war, Indian groups usually sought to settle their own scores against preexisting enemies, and they fought for their own reasons rather than from any blind allegiance to a European government. Indian people also fought wars against Europeans to correct perceived wrongs or to retaliate for attacks by Europeans. Europeans further incited Indians to attack each other or other Europeans by offering rewards for scalps. Indian warriors had always taken war trophies in battle, but Europeans added an economic incentive to the

1730

June 5 Sir Alexander Cumming leads a delegation of Cherokee chiefs to England.

1731

French Louisiana becomes a royal colony in the aftermath of the Natchez Indian revolt.

1733

February 1 The colony of Georgia is founded by James Oglethorpe.

traditional practice. Increasing attacks and the development of a nearly constant state of war in the eighteenth century promoted ever more revenge killings by Indians.

Significant cultural differences between Europeans and Indians had an effect on the way they practiced war. They differed over what constituted murder and over how to respond to killings. Generally, Europeans separated the killing of one human by another into two types: murder, in which case the perpetrator should be punished; and war, which was excusable and did not subject the individual to punishment. For Indians, however, the response to a killing depended on the identity of the murderer. If the killer was an ally or fellow tribe member, negotiations could take place and gifts be paid to the victim's family (sometimes called "covering the dead"). If the killer was a stranger or enemy, revenge killing was called upon by members of the victim's clan against the murderer or a relative of the murderer, which in turn could cause revenge killings from the

American Indians adopted European gun technology to wage war against other Indians and Europeans.

1735

The Comanches displace the Apaches from the southern plains.

1736-1739

Chickasaw-French wars are waged in the lower Mississippi valley. The Chickasaws twice defeat the French armies sent to subdue them.

1737

September 19 The Pennsylvania colony acquires Delaware Indian lands through the deceptive "Walking Purchase."

original murderer's family. These differing ideas about murder caused misunderstandings when, for example, Europeans ended a war and all killing and attacks ceased while Indian people still sought revenge for their dead relatives regardless of whether or not Europeans had called for an end to the war.

Indians in Wars for Empire

Throughout the late seventeenth and eighteenth centuries, the European colonizers of North America frequently warred with one another, and pulled their respective Indian allies and trading partners into the conflicts. The British called these wars the French and Indian Wars, suggesting that the aggressiveness and blame rested solely on the French and their Indian allies. Indians fought on both sides of these wars, however, and the British relied on Indian allies for the fighting in North America as much as the French. Spain also participated in some of these wars on the French side, and their presence in the southeastern portion of the continent meant that their Indian allies also became involved.

King William's War (the War of the Grand Alliance) was fought from 1689 to 1697. In North America, Abenakis from the Northeast fought on the French side while their traditional enemies, the Iroquois, fought on the English side. The Abenakis raided deep into British New England, attacking villages and seizing captives. The Iroquois, especially Mohawks, attacked Algonquian Indian groups and French settlements along the St. Lawrence River. French-allied Algonquin Indians raided the New York settlement of Schenectady in February 1690, killing nearly sixty colonists and burning the town to the ground. French-led attacks also razed Iroquois villages to the ground, persuading the Iroquois to attempt to stay out of future conflicts between their European neighbors.

The War of the Spanish Succession in North America was waged from 1701 to 1713. French troops—together with Abenakis, Christianized Mohawks from the Caughnawaga mission settlement, and Hurons from Lorette—famously raided the New England town of Deerfield, Massachusetts, in February 1704. They seized

Algonquian and other French-allied Indians attacking an English town in Massachusetts.

1738

Smallpox kills half the Cherokee population.

October Frenchman Pierre Gaultier de Varennes, Sieur de La Vérendrye visits Mandan villages along the upper Missouri River from his posts in Canada.

1739

French traders build Fort Cavagnolle on the lower Missouri River.

1741

Vitus Bering opens Russian trade with Native people of the Gulf of Alaska.

sides continued throughout the war. For example, the Mohawks under the command of Sir William Johnson fought for the British. Nearly 2,000 Indians from various Algonquian groups assisted the French in their successful siege of Fort William Henry in New York in 1757 before attacking the retreating British column without French approval, and killing upward of a hundred British troops. The Cherokees began the war as allies of Britain, but British colonists intruded on their lands and ignited Cherokee reprisals. This resulted in the so-called Cherokee War of 1760–61, in which two British armies invaded Cherokee villages and forced them to appeal for peace. This war is also significant for its geopolitical impact: the French decided to vacate North America after their defeat in the Seven Years' War, abandoning their Indian allies to deal with the victorious British on their own.

In addition to being swept into fighting between their European neighbors, American Indians throughout the 1700s fought against Europeans in several wars.

French commander Louis Montcalm trying to prevent Indian attacks on retreating British forces.

1752

June 13 The Logstown Treaty between Virginian and Indian groups in the Ohio valley attempts to prevent conflicts between British colonists and Indians.

1754

June 19–July 11 Albany Congress: several English colonies send representatives to consider Benjamin Franklin's Albany Plan of Union to coordinate relations between the colonies and Indian groups, especially the Iroquois.

July 3 Virginian George Washington is defeated by French and Indian forces at Fort Necessity in Ohio, starting the French and Indian War (the Seven Years' War).

Spanish officials negotiate temporary peace among Comanches, Apaches, and other southwestern Indian groups.

Ever since the French had settled the Gulf Coast at Biloxi in 1699 and then at Mobile, New Orleans, Natchez, and other regions in the early eighteenth century, they had played a tricky diplomatic game of forming strong alliances with some Native groups while waging war on others. From 1712 to 1750, France fought the Mesquakie (Fox) people who opposed French control over the central Mississippi valley. Farther south, French officials decided that they depended on the Choctaws to maintain their own presence in the area. France was unable to supply goods of adequate quantities and quality to all Indian groups in the lower Mississippi valley, so they decided on the Choctaws as the best choice, since theirs was the largest population and the British had alienated them with slave raids by English-allied Indians. The Choctaw-French alliance in turn alienated the Chickasaws, who used their trade with Britain to wage war against France and France's Indian allies along the lower Mississippi River from 1720 to the 1740s.

The Natchez War

The Natchez Indians living along the Mississippi River rebelled against the French presence in 1729. France founded a post among the Natchez Indians in 1714 and soon discovered that the Natchez region comprised some of the best agricultural land in the entire Louisiana colony. In a few short years, hundreds of African slaves lived in and around Natchez on a variety of French farms and plantations. When the Natchez Indians revolted against French

War dance of the Sauks and Foxes. Indian methods of preparing for war involved days of ritual preparation.

1755

Mohawk chief Hendrick calls on the English colonies to select one representative that the Iroquois could meet with rather than numerous separate colonial representatives. He suggests that the English colonies model their confederation on the Iroquois confederation.

April Irish colonist Sir William Johnson becomes the British Superintendent of Indian Affairs for the northern colonies.

July 9 French and Indian forces defeat British General Edward Braddock in the Ohio valley.

September 8 Mohawk leader Hendrick (Tiyanoga) is killed at the Battle of Lake George.

power in 1729 because of French arrogance and offensive behavior, the greatest fear of French government officials and plantation owners was realized: African slaves and Indians had cooperated to attack their French oppressors. On November 28, 1729, this combined force of Indians and Africans killed more than 200 French people. Initially, the French thought that the Natchez Indians had captured the slaves, but many of the "captive" Africans actually assisted the Natchez in beating back the initial counterattacks of the French. This development exposed the danger of encouraging enmity between racial groups. There always existed the possibility that two groups might combine forces to strike back at a third racial group that sought power over them both.

France retaliated against the Natchez and their African allies with massive force, organizing two French military expeditions against them and urging their Choctaw allies to attack the Natchez and capture the Africans. Choctaw chiefs and warriors responded eagerly to the French request because the French had promised them trade goods for each Natchez scalp, and for each former slave captured alive

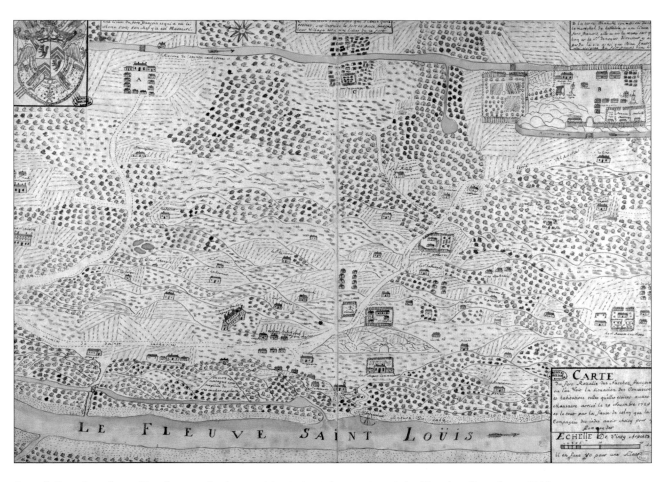

French Fort Rosalie at Natchez on the lower Mississippi River, site of the Natchez Revolt in 1729.

1756–1763

The French and Indian War (the Seven Years' War) between France and Britain draws in eastern Indians on both sides, especially in the Northeast, Ohio valley, and Great Lakes areas.

In the South, Indian groups such as the Choctaws, Chickasaws, Alabamas, Creeks, and Cherokees open a series of diplomatic meetings with each other that bring about peace throughout the region during a time of European war.

and turned over to the French. The combined French and Choctaw attacks decimated the Natchez: dozens were killed, some captives were sold into slavery in Santo Domingo, and survivors were forced to flee to other tribes such as the Chickasaws, Creeks, and Cherokees.

Indian Wars in the Carolinas

While Indians in the Mississippi valley revolted against French control in the early eighteenth century, Indians along the southern Atlantic coast also rebelled against British power. Two factors worked in opposition to good relations between the Carolinians and some of their Indian allies. Since the Carolinians and their Indian allies had wiped out the Spanish mission Indians by 1710, there no longer existed an easily accessible body of Indians to be raided for slaves to sell in the Caribbean. Furthermore, the Indian allies of Carolina encountered crippling trade debts, as they could no longer find captives from other Indian groups or deer herds near the Atlantic coast after several decades of

Natchez Indians with their child, ironically emphasizing the primitiveness and humanity of Indian people.

1758

The Osages attack the Wichitas along the Arkansas River.

April 5 British girl Mary Jemison is captured by the French and Shawnees. She marries a Seneca man and lives among the Senecas for the rest of her life.

The British build Fort Loudon and Fort Prince George among the Cherokees.

1760–1761

War is waged between the Cherokees and the British.

1760–1763

The preachings of Neolin, the Delaware prophet, spread throughout the Ohio valley and the Great Lakes. He calls for militant resistance to British encroachment on their lands.

1763

February 10 The Treaty of Paris ends the Seven Years' War and terminates official French presence in North America, thereby removing a major European ally of dozens of Indian groups.

July 16 British commander Sir Jeffrey Amherst authorizes the distribution of smallpox-infected blankets to Indians in an attempt to reduce Indian enemies of the British.

August 30 Catawba chief King Hagler (Nopkehe) dies.

October 7 The British establish the Royal Proclamation line along the Appalachian Mountains to prevent British colonists from moving farther west and causing conflicts with Indians.

the fur trade had decimated their numbers.

Added to these pressures, a new settlement of a few hundred Swiss and German colonists arrived in eastern North Carolina in 1709. Under the leadership of Baron de Graffenried, the colonists established the town of New Bern in 1710 at the site of a former Tuscarora Indian village. The Tuscaroras, an Iroquoian group by language and culture, had long traded with the colonies of Virginia and South Carolina, but they now faced a sizable, direct, and (according to them) unauthorized incursion into their territory by Europeans. Graffenried and the colonists tried to maintain good relations with the Tuscaroras, but the Indians were determined that the Europeans should leave, arguing that South Carolina did not have permission to sell their lands to other Europeans. The Tuscaroras and their Native allies attacked the Swiss and German colonists on September 22, 1711, and killed nearly 200 settlers.

In response, the British in South Carolina launched two invasions of Tuscarora territory.

....

An attack by Carolinians and Indians against the Tuscarora Indians of North Carolina in 1713.

The first, from 1711 to 1712, was led by Colonel John Barnwell. It included thirty colonists and 500 Indian allies, mainly Yamassees. The Tuscaroras had prepared stout defenses in the form of what the British called the "Tuscarora Fort," complete with breastworks and a high stockade. Barnwell's expedition failed to penetrate the fort's defenses and the fight ended in a stalemate. Barnwell lost money on this largely self-financed expedition because few Indians had been captured for sale as slaves to the British West Indies. Barnwell's goal was less to punish the Tuscaroras for their violence than to use their attack as an excuse to obtain slaves and make money. South Carolina governor James Moore, who had led the English and Indian attacks on the Spanish missions in Florida a decade before, led a new expedition of thirty colonists and 900 Indian allies against the Tuscaroras from 1712 to 1713. Moore's forces laid siege to the Tuscarora Fort and forced its capitulation in March 1713. Nearly a thousand Tuscaroras died, and the British captured and sold 392 of the survivors into slavery in the Caribbean. Most of the remaining Tuscaroras traveled northward and joined distant relatives

among the Iroquois Confederacy, where they formally became the sixth nation of the Iroquois League in 1722. A few stayed in North Carolina on a small reservation.

In 1715 another Indian war against South Carolina nearly destroyed the colony. The Yamassees, long-time partners and fellow slave raiders of the Carolinians, had fallen into deep debt to British fur traders. By 1711 their collective debt equaled 100,000 deerskins. With few nearby Indian groups to raid for captives who could be sold to the British as slaves, the Yamassees found themselves in an untenable situation. Even if there had been enough deer still living near their homes on the coast of South Carolina, they could not hope to kill enough to pay their debts for decades. British fur traders demanded payment anyway and began seizing Yamassee women and children to use as slaves. The Yamassees decided they had no choice but to attack the British, which they did on April 15, 1715. Other Indian groups in the Southeast, especially various Creek Indians, joined the war on the side of the Yamassees and nearly destroyed the South Carolina colony. The Yamassees killed around 400 British

October 10 The British establish a reservation for the Catawbas in South Carolina.

December 13-27 The "Paxton Boys," racist and land-hungry colonists in western Pennsylvania, massacre around twenty Christianized and peaceful Susquehannocks in an unprovoked attack.

1763–1766

Pontiac's Rebellion of several Indian groups occurs against the British in the Ohio valley and Great Lakes.

1764

Alabamas and Coushattas leave villages among the Creeks in Alabama and settle west of the Mississippi River.

February Spanish interests establish St. Louis.

colonists and surrounded the colonial capital at Charles Town. The Carolinians held out, however, and the colony only just survived. When reinforcements arrived, Indians throughout eastern South Carolina were forced to flee or be killed. The British captured hundreds of Yamassees and other Indians and sold them to the Caribbean as slaves.

The well-organized slave-raiding system involving Carolinians and their Native allies fell off dramatically after 1715. One reason was the wars between Carolina and the Tuscarora Indians, and between Carolina and the Yamassee Indians. The Yamassee conflict in 1715 almost destroyed the Carolina colony, and British officials tried to prevent future antagonisms with their Indian allies by limiting the Indian slave trade that had provoked their Yamassee neighbors. However, first they sold hundreds of Tuscarora and Yamassee captives to the Caribbean. South Carolina also constructed a series of new forts to provide places of refuge in case of further Indian attacks.

The death of Pontiac, the Ottawa war chief who helped organize Indian resistance to the British from 1763 to 1765.

The Impact of Constant Warfare on Societies

A state of nearly constant war in the eighteenth century produced significant changes in Indian societies and cultures. Demographically, tribes lost higher than normal numbers of adult males, and Indian women increasingly married men from outside their own communities, diversifying Indian ethnicities and cultures. All Indians continued to struggle against European diseases that threatened their population stability. Economically, Indian groups lost significant numbers of their main providers: adult men did most of the hunting, fishing, and trade. In addition, when Europeans or their Native allies attacked an Indian village, they often burned everything to the ground, including the crops. The resulting poor diets made Indians more susceptible to disease. This loss of crops and the Indians' ability to participate in war with firearms increased their dependency on Europeans for provisions, but Europeans usually cut off supplies at the end of wars because their need for Indian allies had diminished, even though Indian communities still suffered from the effects of war.

Socially, constant war produced changes as Europeans dealt only with men and male leaders

1768

October 24 The Treaty of Fort Stanwix is signed between the Iroquois and the British. The Iroquois cede claims to land south of the Ohio River (Kentucky), even though other Indian groups such as the Shawnees claim the region.

1769

July 16 Spanish Franciscans establish the first mission in California at San Diego. Eventually, twenty-one missions are built from San Diego to San Francisco.

when recruiting allies for war, but that often distorted reality. In many Native groups, such as the Iroquois, women played prominent and decisive roles in deciding when to go to war. The social and political position of men rose as reliance on European goods acquired through trade or as payment in war increased. Growing numbers of refugees and captives changed the makeup of Indian groups, forming new societies. Rituals for war fell into disuse as war became a full-time endeavor. Politically, war chiefs came to dominate both foreign affairs and domestic decisions at the expense of civil chiefs who normally directed domestic affairs. Europeans appealed to younger men as warriors, causing generational splits in Indian communities. Europeans gave warriors medals and greater access to trade goods, enabling them to assert chiefly powers of redistribution and high status. Psychologically, the rapidly changing world created by constant war destroyed a sense of tradition among some Indian groups, and also provided opportunities for a few to assert new leadership roles.

Henry Bouquet negotiates with Ohio valley Indians at the end of Pontiac's Rebellion in 1764.

1774

Virginia governor Lord Dunmore wages war against the Shawnees and Mingos in response to Indian raids on colonists moving into the Kentucky region.

October 10 The Virginian forces win the Battle of Point Pleasant and force Shawnee chiefs to sign a land cession treaty.

The Hudson's Bay Company expands into the Saskatchewan River area, building trade centers.

Shawnee chief Cornstalk leads resistance to Virginian encroachment in the Ohio valley.

Spiritual Revitalization and Militant Resistance

From the end of the Seven Years' War in 1763 until the early nineteenth century, military and cultural resistance on the part of Native Americans became intertwined and inseparable. Powerful movements of resistance resulted when religious and military opposition were combined to overcome Euro-American encroachments and cultural attacks. Religious messages spread by new Indian prophets from this time usually said that Indians had neglected the old ways or corrupted the original meanings of old practices, thereby causing disaster and chaos to enter their world. The solution therefore lay in renewed devotion to traditional beliefs and a militant resistance to Euro-American expansion.

Lappawinsoe, who signed the controversial treaty called the Walking Purchase in Philadelphia in 1737.

The beginnings of such unification among eastern Indians occurred in 1763. That year, the conflict known as "Pontiac's Rebellion" exploded in the Great Lakes area, Ohio valley, and the Northeast. Pontiac was an Ottawa war leader, and the war he nominally led has been traditionally interpreted as an anti-British military movement. And it was, but the spiritual dimension made resistance possible by several groups at once. In 1763, as France (to which most Ohio valley and Great Lakes Indians had allied themselves) relinquished command to the British at the end of the Seven Years' War, British officers refused to continue the French practice of giving annual gifts to tribes and mediating disputes. Indians interpreted this action as arrogance, and many thought the British sought to destroy Indians altogether. They wondered how they would hunt and

Two Ottawa chiefs from the Michilimackinac area of Lake Huron.

trade for supplies if they did not receive ammunition, guns, and people to repair the guns. Amid this ongoing crisis, a new spiritual leader and message became popular.

A Delaware Indian named Neolin claimed to have the ability to communicate with the "Master of Life." He said he had received a

1775

March 14 The Treaty of Sycamore Shoals is signed; Richard Henderson's land purchase from the Cherokees.

A group of Cherokees settles along the St. Francis River in Arkansas.

1775–1783

Fighting in the American Revolution pulls in eastern Indian groups on both sides as the British and the Americans vie for their allegiance.

Indian groups, including the Catawbas, Oneidas, Tuscaroras, and Stockbridges, assist the Americans during the war.

1776–1778

Captain James Cook begins British trade with northwestern coast people.

vision from heaven, where there were no white people, only Indians. He preached that the Indians had once had direct access to heaven, but that since the coming of the whites, they had been taught sins and vices that barred their way and diverted them to hell. He urged a return to traditional Indian customs, even to the point of giving up guns for bows and arrows. Indians, Neolin said, had to live without any trade or connections to white people and must clothe and support themselves as their ancestors had. He preached that all Indians had a common destiny, and eastern Indians began to see themselves as having a common enemy in Europeans, especially the British. Tribal differences became less important, especially within the context of the multiethnic communities that had formed in the Ohio valley as a result of warfare and migrations. Neolin recognized whites as a source of Indian problems, but he believed that the core of the problems lay with the Indians themselves. Therefore, they could correct the problems by returning to traditional spiritual beliefs, participating in certain rituals, and living properly. To take the blame for their own

Fort Harmar, site of a treaty between the United States government and the Delaware, Potawatomi, Wyandot, and Sauk tribes in 1789, which ceded land between the Mississippi River and the Ohio Territory.

1777

August 6 The Battle of Oriskany marks the permanent split of the Iroquois Confederacy during the American Revolution as Oneidas and Tuscaroras battle on the American side against Mohawks, and other Iroquois on the British side.

Oneida, Tuscarora, and Delaware Indians assist American troops during the winter at Valley Forge.

Mohawk leader Joseph Brant leads pro-British Iroquois against American and Indian forces. Brant is the brother-in-law of British Indian agent Sir William Johnson.

October 10 Shawnee chief Cornstalk is murdered by American soldiers at Fort Randolph, West Virginia, while under a flag of truce. This action convinces the Shawnees to fight against the Americans.

predicaments enabled Indians to take control; those who changed and followed Neolin's teachings could reassert power over their lives.

Pontiac adopted Neolin's spiritual message (as did many others) and began organizing a pan-Indian movement around it. Pontiac accepted Neolin's moral teachings and added an anti-British (rather than just anti-European) theme. Indians throughout the Great Lakes area flocked to Neolin's village to hear his advice. Many of them altered his teachings to a more Christian interpretation or a less Christian one. Others, like Pontiac, saw no need to get rid of all the white man's technology, especially guns. Pontiac traveled throughout the region, enlisting support

United States forces under General Anthony Wayne finally defeated the Ohio valley Indians led by Little Turtle at the Battle of Fallen Timbers on August 20, 1794.

1778

September 17 Delaware chief White Eyes signs a treaty with the United States at Fort Pitt, Pennsylvania, and is an outspoken ally, but is later murdered by American colonists.

The first treaty between the United States and an Indian group is signed at Fort Pitt with the Delawares.

November The death of White Eyes convinces most Delawares to renounce the alliance with the Americans and instead support the British.

for his planned rebellion. Thousands of Indians joined from virtually every tribe north of the Ohio River and east of the Mississippi River, including the Delawares, Ottawas, Senecas, Shawnees, Chippewas, Wyandots, Weas, Miamis, and Potawatomis. The militants laid siege to Detroit and captured nine British forts in the Great Lakes and Ohio valley. The sieges lasted two to three years, but Detroit did not fall. The British eventually counterattacked and fought the Indians to a stalemate. The fighting died down temporarily, and the British government issued the 1763 proclamation that told their colonists to remain east of the Appalachian Mountains, away from Indian lands, in an attempt to prevent further conflict. Unfortunately, the proclamation was nearly impossible to enforce and tensions between colonists and Indians remained high.

A Contest of Cultures

As Neolin's movement suggests, the battle for the minds and spirits of Indians and European

Mohican Samson Occom (1726–1792) went to England in 1766 to raise money for founding Dartmouth College.

colonists grew in the eighteenth century. For example, in New England Reverend Eleazer Wheelock, inspired by the Great Awakening, founded Moor's Indian Charity School in Lebanon, Connecticut, in 1754. Like John Eliot's attempts at Indian conversion a century earlier, the British still insisted on the separation of Indian children from their parents and culture in order to become Christian. Wheelock's most well-known Indian convert was a Mohegan man named Samson Occom, who studied with Wheelock in the 1740s. Occom became literate, trained as a minister, and traveled to England from 1764 to 1765. However, toward the end of his life, his assessment of his British education and conversion to Christianity left him embittered because no congregation of British New Englanders would accept him as their minister because he was an Indian. If Occom, who had completely transformed his culture and lifestyle to match colonial New England, was not accepted as an equal British citizen, it was fair to ask if *any* Indian would ever be accepted as an equal in British society. In 1769 Wheelock's school moved to Hanover, New Hampshire, and eventually became Dartmouth

1779

April–September American General John Sullivan leads an invasion against the Iroquois Indians. The invasion forces nearly all Iroquois people to flee their homes and creates a refugee crisis at British Fort Niagara.

1779–1781

On the Gulf Coast, Spain and Britain compete for Indian allies as they fight each other during the American Revolution in battles at Mobile and Pensacola.

Choctaws, Creeks, and Chickasaws come to the aid of Britain along the Gulf Coast.

College. There were many other Christian missionary groups converting Indians in the eighteenth century, but despite their doctrinal differences, all European missionaries sought to undermine Indian religion and culture and turn Indians into imitations of Europeans.

White Indians

Perhaps the most successful group in the contest of cultures was the Indians. As a colonial farmer said in the eighteenth century, "Thousands of Europeans are Indians and we have no examples of even one of those Aborigines having from choice become Europeans!" Benjamin Franklin wondered in 1753 how it was that "when an Indian child has been brought up among us, taught our language and habituated to our customs, yet if he goes to see his relations and makes one Indian Ramble with them, there is no perswading [sic] him ever to return . . . [But] when white persons of either sex have been taken prisoners young by the Indians, and lived awhile among them, tho' ransomed by their friends, and treated with all imaginable tenderness to prevail with them to stay among

the English, yet in a short time they become disgusted with our manner of life, and the care and pains that are necessary to support it, and take the first good opportunity of escaping again into the woods, from whence there is no reclaiming them."

Europeans became Indians voluntarily by running away to Indian communities, by choosing not to escape when captured by Indians, or by opting to remain with their new Indian relations after being captured despite being offered the chance to return home as the result of a peace treaty. Emotional attachments between captives and Indians were often strong. For example, after defeating Delaware, Shawnee, and Seneca Indians at Bushy Run in 1763 during Pontiac's Rebellion, British Colonel Henry Bouquet ordered that all white captives and any children of white captives be returned to the British. The children came only by kicking and screaming and being forced by

Benjamin Franklin commented on the willingness of Europeans to join Indian societies and the unwillingness of Indians to join European society.

1779–1783

A massive smallpox epidemic extends from Mexico to Canada.

1780

The Blackfeet Confederacy begins to displace Shoshones from northern Montana.

Mandan and Hidatsa villages unite along the upper Missouri River.

Prominent eighteenth-century Cherokee chief Attakullakulla dies.

their adopted Indian parents, holding on to their Indian parents' legs and refusing to be taken to the British. Many of the captives had lived with the Indians for several years and had forgotten their original language. Several female prisoners had chosen Indian husbands and refused to leave them or their children. European women who had taken Indian husbands and had children with them were often not accepted back into European society, providing an additional incentive to stay. Indian life was attractive to many Europeans and Americans. Two adult eighteenth-century converts explained that they preferred Indian society for "the most perfect freedom, the ease of living, and the absence of those cares and corroding solicitudes which so often prevail with us."

Making Treaties

Ever since Europeans first arrived in North America, treaties had been negotiated with Indians, but the frequency of such negotiations

European captives of Ohio valley Indians resisting return to the British at the end of Pontiac's Rebellion in 1764.

1782

March 8 At the Gnadenhutten Massacre, Pennsylvania militiamen attack the Moravian mission at Gnadenhutten and massacre ninety-six Delaware Indians.

Cherokee leader Dragging Canoe moves his followers, the Chickamaugas, to the Tennessee River.

Renowned Cherokee leader Oconostota dies.

increased considerably in the eighteenth century as constant war necessitated constant meetings. When Europeans and Indians met in treaty negotiations, they brought different diplomatic traditions and expectations to the encounter. Both sides wanted to accomplish specific goals, such as ending conflicts, but both also wanted to maintain their separate identities and control over their own actions. Europeans sought to establish in written treaties their dominance over Indian groups. Indians usually dealt from a position of equality with Europeans or sometimes felt they were the superior power in the negotiations. Indians and Europeans negotiated treaties for several reasons, including satisfying trade debts, European desires for Indian land, and Indian hopes that land sales would stop white encroachment on their remaining lands and to end wars. Treaties locked both sides into commitments and obligations, requiring the performance of rituals.

The customs of Indian diplomacy meant that Europeans had to learn new diplomatic

The American Revolution established the United States as the primary Euro-American power.

1783

May 31 Creek Indians sign the Treaty of Augusta with Georgia for a land cession.

After 1783, the United States was the only major Euro-American power throughout most of eastern North America, forcing Indian groups to resist or cooperate with American demands.

September 3 The Treaty of Paris ends the Revolutionary War and grants recognition of United States independence. Indian allies of Britain are not provided for.

behaviors. Treaties were invalid in Indian eyes unless the calumet (sometimes called the "peace pipe") was smoked and gifts were exchanged. Many Indian groups also required that the European diplomats be metaphorically adopted before trade could commence. Such rituals made the agreement sacred, in which none of the parties were to break the provisions, and they turned potential enemies into friends and kin. Treaty negotiations lasted days and sometimes included dozens of Indian speakers. Mnemonic devices such as wampum belts provided Indians with a visual record of what had transpired, whereas Europeans and Americans relied on the signed treaty document for their records.

Many potential problems arose from treaty negotiations between Europeans and Indians. Language was always an issue, as both sides relied on interpreters who may have had a limited understanding of what was said. Some interpreters purposely misled one side or the other in pursuit of their own agenda. Europeans sometimes altered the written treaty from what had been verbally expressed and agreed to. Most Indians in the colonial and early national period could not read and so were unable to identify when a written document had misquoted them. Another recurrent issue was whether or not the Indians who signed a treaty were authorized by the tribe to do so. In addition, Indian signatures on a treaty did not always mean they agreed to its provisions. Several treaties negotiated in the 1700s remained disputed by one side or the other, fueling tension and conflict between Indians and Europeans.

A Chippewa pipe, indicative of calumets in Indian diplomacy that required European negotiators to smoke.

United States–Indian Relations

From the beginning of the American Revolution in 1775, Indians were a primary concern of the United States government. At first, both the British and the Americans tried to keep all Indians neutral in the conflict. As the war became a fight for American independence, both sides quickly changed their stance toward Indians and vied for allies. Most Ohio valley and northeastern Indians fought for the British. The Cherokees attacked Carolina settlers and had their villages invaded by four separate American armies. Their cultural relatives, the Iroquois, also suffered disaster in the American Revolution, with most Iroquois, especially the Mohawks under Joseph Brant, fighting for the British, while the Oneidas and Tuscaroras took the American side and attacked other Iroquois at the Battle of Oriskany in 1777. American armies under General John Sullivan invaded Iroquois country in 1779, burning villages and crops to the ground. Indian groups siding with the Americans in the war included the Oneidas, Tuscaroras, Stockbridges (of Massachusetts), Micmacs, Passamaquoddies,

1784

June–July Southern Indian groups sign treaties with Spain.

October 22 The second Treaty of Fort Stanwix is signed with the Iroquois. The United States demands nearly all Iroquois land in New York.

After the American Revolution, one Iroquois Confederacy exists in New York and another across the border in Canada.

Penobscots (of Maine and Nova Scotia), and the Catawbas from the Carolinas. Delaware Indians in the Ohio valley had declared neutrality, but after the Gnadenhutten Massacre of converted pacifist Moravian Delawares by Pennsylvania settlers in 1782, they fought against the Americans. In the South, most Indian groups supported the British in their attempt to defend Mobile and Pensacola from Spanish attack, but ultimately Spain won and took the entire Gulf Coast under their control.

Early American relations with Indians were based on acquiring land with honor. The new government had virtually no money after the end of the war, but it needed to pay soldiers from the revolution with land. The problem was that Indians possessed that land. The Treaty of Paris, which ended the American Revolution in 1783, did not mention Indians at all.

....

Left: U.S. Major General John Sullivan, who led the American invasion of the Iroquois in New York in 1779.

Right: The Treaty of Paris in 1783 ended the American Revolution, but failed to mention Indians.

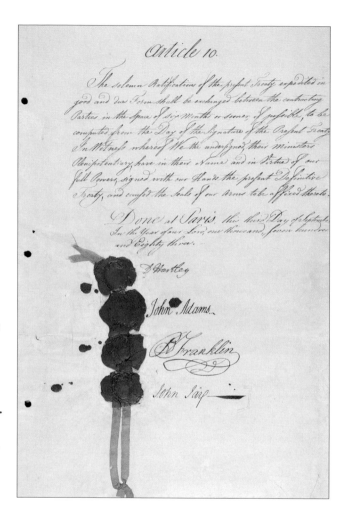

1785

January 21 The Treaty of Fort McIntosh is signed with Wyandots, Delawares, Chippewas, and Ottawas: the United States gains lands in Tennessee, Pennsylvania, Ohio, and Indiana.

November 12 An unauthorized group of Creek Indians signs the Treaty of Galphinton with Georgia.

1785–1786

November–January The Treaties of Hopewell between the United States and southern Indian groups establishes formal relations between the United States and the Cherokees, Choctaws, and Chickasaws.

1786

Spanish New Mexico governor Juan Bautista de Anza makes peace with the Comanches.

Early U.S. Indian Policy

The United States had to develop its own ideas and tactics to deal with Indians, most of whom had not been defeated in the war. American officials were aware that the rest of the world watched them closely to see if the democratic and human rights principles enshrined in the Declaration of Independence would be extended to the Native people within the new country's boundaries. The United States had three possible ways of acquiring Indian land: it could invade Indian country and seize the land, or negotiate treaties to get land cessions from Indians, or "civilize" Indian people and turn them into individual landowners and Americans. The first strategy of going to war was the least favored because war was expensive and risked bringing the condemnation of Europe. Therefore, for the first few years after the American Revolution, the focus of the U.S. government toward Indians turned to treaties and "civilization."

Early U.S. treaties with Indians reflected the "right of conquest" tactic of seizing Indian lands. The United States felt that, by defeating Britain and her allies, it could dictate to tribes the terms of settlement, including land cessions. For

The signing of the Declaration of Independence in July 1776 launched the new United States of America and started the era of U.S.-Indian relations.

1787

July 13 The Northwest Ordinance is passed by the Continental Congress. It organizes American expansion into what is now the Midwest.

1789

The U.S. Constitution grants Congress sole power to regulate commerce with Indians and prohibits states from negotiating treaties with Indian groups.

Under the U.S. Constitution, Congress assigns responsibility for Indian affairs to the War Department.

A depiction of the transfer of the Louisiana Territory from French to American control, which placed millions of acres of Indian land under the ostensible control of the United States.

example, the 1784 Treaty of Fort Stanwix with the Iroquois was made with little negotiation, and the terms were provided by U.S. officials. The Oneidas and Tuscaroras were promised protection of their lands for siding with the United States during the war, whereas the other Iroquois ceded thousands of acres to the United States. The Iroquois felt that they had little choice but to settle since their people were experiencing near starvation caused by the destruction of their villages, and a refugee crisis brought about by Iroquois people fleeing the violence. Similarly, in the 1785 Treaty of Fort McIntosh with the Wyandots, Delawares, Chippewas, Ottawas, and other groups, the United States insisted that the Indians had to provide them with hostages until all American captives had been returned. In these treaties and the one with the Shawnees at Fort Finney in 1786, the United States set up "reserves" for these tribes on which non-Indians were not permitted to settle, but the United States also forced them into land cessions. These treaties led to the United States acquiring undisputed title for some western lands, but Indian people did not always agree that the treaties were valid.

1790

July 22 The first Trade and Intercourse Act is passed by the U.S. Congress to regulate trade with Indians and further define and establish national government authority in Indian affairs.

October General Josiah Harmar and the U.S. Army are defeated by an Indian confederation in the Ohio valley.

The Miami chief Little Turtle and the Shawnee chief Blue Jacket organize militant resistance to U.S. expansion into the Ohio valley.

August 17 The Treaty of New York between the United States and the Creek Indians commits the United States to protect Creek sovereignty and creates a formal relationship between the two groups.

Creek leader Alexander McGillivray travels from the South to New York City to negotiate with the United States on behalf of his people.

1787 Northwest Ordinance

Still operating under the Articles of Confederation, the government began putting all Indian affairs under its control with the 1787 Northwest Ordinance. The ordinance set up the system to form new territories and states out of lands beyond the boundaries of the thirteen original states. The act committed the United States to western expansion, but it stated that Indian lands could be seized only in warfare authorized by Congress and not by states or individuals. The wording sounded generous to Indians, but it provided a way for the United States to still get Indian lands: "The utmost good faith shall always be observed towards the Indians; their lands and property shall never be taken from them without their consent; and in their property, rights, and liberty, they shall never be invaded or disturbed, unless in just and lawful wars authorized by Congress; but laws founded in justice and humanity shall from time to time be made, for preventing wrongs being done to them, and for preserving peace and friendship with them."

Fort Stanwix in Rome, New York, where treaties were negotiated with the Iroquois in 1784.

1790–1795

War breaks out between the United States and Ohio valley Indians.

Congress and President Washington wage war on Indians in the Ohio valley in an attempt to gain title to lands there and open the area for American settlement.

The war with the Ohio valley Indians, sometimes called "Little Turtle's War" after the Miami chief who leads some of the Indian forces, dominates George Washington's terms as president.

President George Washington at his home, Mount Vernon. Washington implemented the "civilization" policy that hoped to bring Indians into American society.

1791

July 2 Cherokees sign the Treaty of Holston with the United States.

November 4 The Ohio valley Indian confederation defeats a second U.S. Army led by General Arthur St. Clair in the U.S. Army's greatest loss to Indians.

1791–1794

George Vancouver trades with Indian people on the northwestern Pacific coast.

In 1789, under the new constitution, the U.S. government placed Indian affairs under the War Department in the executive branch. Therefore, the government viewed Indians as enemies whom they would constantly have to fight in order to acquire lands. Not until 1824 was the Bureau of Indian Affairs formed as a separate department, and in 1849 it was placed under the jurisdiction of the Department of the Interior, where it remains today. In the 1790 Indian Trade and Intercourse Act, the government declared that only traders licensed by Congress were allowed to trade with Indians; states could not issue trade licenses. The Intercourse Act also stated that only sales of Indian lands that were approved by Congress were legal and that Indians could not sell lands to states or to individual Americans.

Almost as soon as the new government was elected, war with Indians erupted in the Ohio valley. This area was a mix of numerous tribes living in villages containing members of various groups. Most Ohio valley Indians opposed dictation of terms by the U.S. government and the expansion of American settlements into the region. The multitribal militant resistance movement was led by the Miami war chief Little Turtle and the Shawnee war chief Blue Jacket.

Pacifying the Tribes

In 1790 President George Washington sent General Josiah Harmar to the Ohio valley to pacify those tribes that opposed U.S. expansion. Harmar's army consisted of 1,100 Pennsylvanian, Virginian, and Kentucky militia, and 300 federal regulars. In September, the multitribal Indian forces routed Harmar's army in two separate attacks. Washington considered this an embarrassing defeat and replaced Harmar with General Arthur St. Clair. St. Clair's army of 2,000 six-month enlistees marched into the Ohio valley in 1791. Many of his men deserted due to a lack of provisions, no pay, and inadequate training. Indian warriors under the leadership of Little Turtle and Blue Jacket obliterated the American soldiers and sent the survivors fleeing for their lives, leaving their supplies and weapons behind. The Indians killed around 600 U.S. soldiers

Miami war chief Little Turtle (1752–1812) led the armed Indian resistance to American expansion in the 1790s.

1793

The Hudson's Bay Company builds the Brandon trading house among the Assiniboines in Manitoba.

1794

August 20 General Anthony Wayne finally defeats the Ohio valley Indian confederation at the Battle of Fallen Timbers in northern Ohio.

November 8 Chickamauga Cherokees make peace with the United States.

1795

August 3 The Treaty of Greenville ends the war between the United States and the Ohio valley Indian confederacy, which cedes most of Ohio to the United States.

French trader Auguste Chouteau builds Fort Carondelet among the Osages in Kansas.

and wounded another 300, while suffering only twenty-one casualties. This was the largest defeat of a U.S. Army unit at the hands of Indians. Making their message clear regarding land, the Indians stuffed the mouths of dead soldiers with dirt. This huge victory was, however, short-lived.

General "Mad" Anthony Wayne

In 1792 Washington appointed a new general named "Mad" Anthony Wayne to wage war against the Ohio valley Indians. Wayne planned his strategy, taking a year to train recruits in guerrilla warfare tactics to enable them to fight Indians on an equal footing. His army, which numbered 3,000 troops under long-term enlistments, possessed better equipment than their defeated predecessors, and Wayne requested that they construct a series of resupply forts from the Ohio River north up to the Great Lakes across what is now Ohio. On June 29, 1794, Little Turtle's forces attacked Wayne's army at the site of

Inauguration of George Washington, who oversaw a major war against Ohio valley Indians in the 1790s.

1796

U.S. Congress establishes government trading factories.

April 16 Mohawk woman Molly Brant, the sister of Joseph Brant and wife of William Johnson, dies.

June 1 Tennessee becomes a state.

1797

September 16 With the Treaty of Big Tree, Iroquois reservations are established in western New York and Ontario.

The American Philosophical Society of Philadelphia expands its focus to the archaeological remains of Indian people, especially Indian mounds in the East.

their previous victory over St. Clair, but this time the battle ended in a stalemate. Little Turtle then tried to appeal for peace to save lives and keep the confederacy intact, but most of his warriors disagreed and attacked Wayne's army again. The decisive battle happened at Fallen Timbers in northern Ohio on August 20, 1794. This time, the Americans drove the Indians from the field and inflicted greater damage, with hundreds of Indians and only thirty-eight Americans dead. Indian survivors fled to British Fort Miami, but the British refused to open the gates and ignite conflict with the United States. Wayne ordered the destruction of Indian villages and crops as punishment, and then he negotiated the Treaty of Greenville in 1795 that forced the Indians to cede nearly all of present-day Ohio and part of Indiana to the United States. Little Turtle and Blue Jacket signed the treaty, but younger warriors refused to abide by it and regrouped to fight another day.

The Treaty of Greenville in 1795 ceded Ohio to the United States after the defeat of the Ohio Valley Indian Confederacy.

1798

April 7 Congress creates the Mississippi Territory, which later becomes the states of Mississippi and Alabama.

1799

Seneca prophet Handsome Lake has a spiritual vision that spawns the Longhouse religion among the Iroquois.

The Russian-American Company is set up to monopolize the fur trade in Alaska for Russia.

1800–1900

The nineteenth century brought tremendous change to Indian communities throughout North America. At the start of the century, a young United States of America and a still-British Canada tried to extend their limited power to the Mississippi River and the West.

B y the end of the eighteenth century, the United States and the new nation of Canada were industrial powers that stretched from the Atlantic to the Pacific, and no longer saw Indians as a possible impediment to national expansion.

The century began with a joining of religious revitalization and military resistance under the auspices of two Shawnee Indians, Tecumseh and Tenskwatawa. The Shawnees had had a

Left: A portrayal of the Battle of the Thames, where Tecumseh was killed, October 5, 1813.
Right: Tecumseh (1768–1813), along with his brother Tenskwatawa, organized the massive Ohio valley pan-Indian resistance movement.

migratory background since Europeans arrived on the continent and claimed they "had always been the frontier." Tecumseh and Tenskwatawa's family had lived among the Creeks in the South and, by the late eighteenth century, bands of Shawnees lived in the Ohio valley, in the South, west of the Mississippi River, and everywhere in between. The Shawnees enjoyed a reputation for constant opposition to white expansion, and other tribes respected them for that reason.

In 1805 Tenskwatawa had a vision that enabled him to communicate with the Great Spirit. The message spread by Tenskwatawa, who was known as the "Shawnee Prophet" after this event, called

on Indians to avoid alcohol, treat elders and the sick with respect, and remain faithful to their spouses. Tenskwatawa also commanded warriors to have only one wife. He drew clear distinctions between Indian and white worlds, and encouraged Indians to cut all ties with whites. He blamed shamans (accusing many of them of being witches) and older chiefs for the troubles the Indians were experiencing in the early nineteenth century, and sought a return to traditional values while changing many of those values to fit the times. He denounced some traditional dances and ceremonies while offering new ones to replace them, providing a sense of renewal, and purging the old evil ways. He also renounced individualism and sought a return to community values. Tenskwatawa attracted thousands of followers from dozens of tribes, and they constructed Prophet's Town at Tippecanoe in Indiana.

Tenskwatwa's brother Tecumseh used the message of spiritual revitalization to build a military resistance movement against the United States. He traveled from the Great Lakes to the South to spread his brother's message and persuade Indians to join Prophet's Town.

In 1811, while Tecumseh was visiting southern Indians, William Henry Harrison, governor of the Indiana Territory, attacked Prophet's Town at Tippecanoe to try to stop any possibility of an Indian attack on Americans. Harrison had learned to be wary of Tecumseh and his brother. Two years before, in 1809, Harrison had tricked a group of Indians without tribal authority to cede three million acres in Indiana for alcohol, $7,000, and a small annuity. Tecumseh confronted Harrison with a thousand warriors and demanded that the treaty be voided. Despite almost coming to blows, Harrison did not invalidate the treaty, and enmity simmered between him and the Shawnee leaders. The Shawnee prophet had told his followers at Prophet's Town that they would be immune to bullets. Harrison actually lost more troops in the battle than the Indians, but faith in the Shawnee prophet was shaken and some followers left.

Tenskwatawa inspired Native people to join in a new cultural and militaristic resistance movement against the United States.

1800

The Comanches and Kiowas form an alliance.

October 1 Spain retrocedes Louisiana to France.

1802

May 23 Tlingit Indians in Alaska destroy the Russian-American Company's primary trading post at Sitka.

1803

April 30 The Louisiana Purchase from France doubles the land claimed by the United States and brings the United States into contact with dozens of Indian groups in the West.

1804

The Lewis and Clark expedition explores the new Louisiana territory. The Americans encounter numerous Indian groups in the upper plains.

1804–1806 The Lewis and Clark expedition winters among the Mandans and along the Columbia River to the northwestern coast, establishing the first contacts between Americans and many western tribes.

1805

1805–1806 Teenage Shoshone woman Sacajawea, who is married to a French trader named Toussaint Charbonneau, acts as a guide, translator, and diplomat for the Lewis and Clark expedition.

1805–1811 Shawnee prophet Tenskwatawa preaches a new religion of spiritual revitalization among Ohio Valley and Great Lakes Indians.

1805–1811 Tenskwatawa's brother Tecumseh turns this religious message into a political movement opposed to American expansion, and attempts to unite all the tribes east of the Mississippi River.

At the Battle of Tippecanoe on November 7, 1811, Indian forces under Tenskwatawa attacked, but were repulsed by U.S. forces under William Henry Harrison.

1807

November 24 Mohawk leader Joseph Brant dies.

1808

The American Fur Company is started by John Jacob Astor.

1809

September 30 The fraudulent Treaty of Fort Wayne, signed by supposed leaders of the Munsees, Delawares, and Potawatomis, cedes 3 million acres to the United States.

1810

Some Cherokees begin to migrate to Arkansas.

1811

Tecumseh travels to the South to meet Indian groups and seek their aid in combating the United States.

The Choctaws reject Tecumseh's message of militant resistance to the Americans, but a significant segment of the Creeks adopt a similar stance.

November 7 At the Battle of Tippecanoe, forces under William Henry Harrison, governor of the Northwest Territory, defeat Indian forces massed at Tenskwatawa's village.

Indians in the Ohio valley continued small-scale attacks on American settlers, which was one reason among many why the United States declared war on Britain—the Americans blamed Britain for encouraging Indian resistance.

The War of 1812

Once the War of 1812 began, the British needed Indian support because many of their regular troops were tied up in Europe, fighting in the Napoleonic wars. Tecumseh and his brother joined the British in declaring war on the United States, and Indian forces and the British soon took Detroit and Fort Dearborn. The British made Tecumseh a brigadier general for his success

....

Left: William Henry Harrison (1773–1841).

Right: The death of Tecumseh at the Battle of the Thames in 1813.

in fighting the Americans in the early stages of the war. After losing the Great Lakes in a naval battle, the British pulled back to Canada with Tecumseh and Indian warriors protecting the retreat. The U.S. Army pursued them and they fought a battle along the Thames River on October 5, 1813, which resulted in Tecumseh's death. With his death, the hopes of many Indians for an Indian confederacy also died. However, Indians continued to fight the United

1812

Louisiana becomes a state.

Thomas Selkirk establishes a colony called the Red River Settlement in Canada.

1812–1814 Civil war breaks out among the Creek Indians in Alabama as traditionalist Red Sticks wage war on Creeks who have adopted some of the behaviors and values of the Americans.

1812–1815 The War of 1812 is fought between Britain and the United States, with Tecumseh and other Ohio valley and Great Lakes Indians fighting against the Americans.

1813

Virginia breaks up the Gingaskin reservation on the eastern shore.

August 30 Red Stick Creeks attack Fort Mims in Alabama and kill more than 350 Americans and non–Red Stick Creeks.

October 5 Tecumseh is killed in battle on the Thames River in Canada.

1814

March 27 Battle of Horseshoe Bend on the Tallapoosa River, where Americans, Cherokees, Choctaws, and non–Red Stick Creeks defeat the Red Stick Creeks.

August 9 The Treaty of Fort Jackson ends the Creek War and results in a large land cession to the United States.

States in the South. A division of Creek Indians called the Red Sticks followed the prophet Hidlis Hadjo and attacked acculturated Creeks and Americans. In August 1813, the Red Sticks attacked Fort Mims near Mobile, Alabama, killing nearly 250 acculturated Creeks and Americans. The U.S. government ordered General Andrew Jackson of Tennessee to Alabama with militia forces from Kentucky and Tennessee, along with Indian allies, including other Creeks, Choctaws, and Cherokees. In March 1814, the bulk of the Red Sticks died at the hands of these soldiers at the Battle of the Horseshoe Bend on the Tallapoosa River. In the Treaty of Fort Jackson signed after the battle, the Creek Nation, including Creek allies of the United States, ceded 14 million acres to the United States. Surviving Red Sticks joined their relatives among the Seminoles in Florida and continued to fight against U.S. expansion during the 1850s.

U.S.-Seminole War

On May 9, 1832, a removal treaty was signed between the United States and the Seminole Indians at Payne's Landing in northeastern Florida.

A militant faction of the Creek Indians called the "Red Sticks" attacked Fort Mims in Alabama on August 30, 1813, killing other Creeks and some Americans, and sparking an American invasion of their lands.

1815

January 8 Andrew Jackson leads forces, including some Choctaw Indians, which defeat the British at the Battle of New Orleans.

August 10 The Seneca prophet Handsome Lake dies.

1817

December 10 Mississippi becomes a state.

July 18 The Selkirk Treaty is signed in lower Manitoba, in which Canada cedes Indian land.

1817–1818 The First Seminole War takes place between the United States and the Seminole Indians as Andrew Jackson invades Spanish Florida.

The Cherokees establish a written constitution.

Florida settlers had long complained about Indian depredations committed by the Seminoles, and Georgia plantation owners protested that runaway slaves found refuge among these Florida Indians. Combined with a devastating drought and near-starvation in 1831, Seminole representatives signed the treaty in order to relieve their suffering. This treaty stipulated that removal was conditioned on the Seminoles agreeing to settle in the western territory that the War Department had chosen for them. Under duress, the seven Seminoles who journeyed west to inspect their new land signed a new

Tuko-See-Mathla, a Seminole chief of the early nineteenth century.

removal treaty with American agents at Fort Gibson on March 28, 1833. The treaty declared that the Seminoles agreed with the location of their new lands, accepted political unification with the Creek Indians, and assented to immediate emigration.

On their return to Florida, the Seminole agents renounced the Fort Gibson Treaty as coerced and the Seminoles refused to abide by the stipulations of either treaty. This impasse resulted in a bitter, drawn-out war, often referred to as the Second Seminole War. It began in 1835 and did not end until 1842, when all but a fraction of the Seminoles had been killed or forcibly removed. Pockets of Seminoles and their African American brethren remained in Florida, however, and their descendants are still there.

Indian Removal and Land Cessions, 1830 to 1848

The Indian removal policy implemented by the U.S.

An attack by Seminole Indians on an American fort during the Second Seminole War of 1835–1842.

government in the early nineteenth century resulted in numerous land cession treaties with Indian groups east of the Mississippi River. Under the removal policy, treaties were negotiated with eastern tribes, including the Choctaws, Chickasaws, Creeks, Cherokees, and the Seminoles in the South, and more than twenty tribes in New York, the Great Lakes area, and along the Mississippi River north of the Ohio River. These treaties ceded millions of acres of land to American control and forced the relocation of tens of thousands of Indians to the Indian Territory.

1818

U.S. Congress appoints federal agents to deal with Indian tribes.

1819

February 22 The United States acquires Florida from Spain, initiating American expansion into the region and conflicts between Americans and Seminoles.

1820–1823

Americans begin settling in eastern Texas, and conflicts soon develop between them and Indians living in the area.

1821

August 10 Missouri becomes a state.

September 27 Mexico wins independence from Spain.

The Cherokee man Sequoyah invents the Cherokee syllabary, the first Indian-created written language in North America.

1823

Virginia breaks up the Nottoway Indian reservation.

Origins of the Removal Policy

The U.S. government policy that removed Indian groups east of the Mississippi River to the Indian Territory in the first half of the nineteenth century had many causes. From the beginning of the United States under the new constitution in 1789, government officials proposed eventual Indian removal. In 1789 Secretary of War Henry Knox suggested the inevitability of removal, asserting that "in a short period the idea of an Indian this side of the Mississippi will be found only in the pages of the historian." One component of early U.S. Indian policy, which began under President George Washington and continued under his successors until President Andrew Jackson, was the civilization plan. According to this program, the U.S. government urged Indian peoples to adopt American notions of economy, politics, and gender roles. This meant that Indians should abandon hunting as a source of sustenance for agriculture, especially the production of cash crops like cotton. Differing views about the proper use of land divided Indians and Euro-Americans from the earliest days of contact, and eastern Indians pointed out that they already grew vast quantities of corn, squash, beans, pumpkins, and sunflowers. Indian men hunted deer and other animals to provide meat protein in their families' diets and to engage in the fur trade that the U.S. government tried to manipulate. Indian women farmed among the matrilineal eastern tribes and Indian men tended to view such work as "women's work," in contrast with American understandings of gender roles. The U.S. civilization policy sought to turn Indian men into farmers and Indian women into spinners and weavers of cotton, thereby challenging Indian cultural concepts at a basic level. In addition—and more to the point of land cessions—the U.S. government insisted that Indians who no longer hunted required far less land and so should sell their excess to the United States, to be sold in turn to Euro-American settlers. Indians greeted the

General Henry Knox (1750–1806) served as U.S. Secretary of War under President George Washington.

1824

February 21 Chumash Indians revolt against Mexican Catholic missions in Southern California.

March 11 The U.S. Secretary of War creates a Bureau of Indian Affairs within the War Department.

1825

August 19 The Treaty of Prairie du Chien established peace among western Great Lakes tribes.

1826

Albert Gallatin publishes *A Table of Indian Languages of the United States.*

The Choctaws establish a written constitution.

1827

Cherokees in Georgia adopt a written constitution modeled on the U.S. Constitution.

June 27 The Red Bird Uprising (the Winnebago War) occurs among Ho-Chunks in Wisconsin against local American settlers and militias. It is lead by Winnebago and Sauk prophet White Cloud and promotes traditional values and culture.

civilization plan with mixed reactions. A minority of elite and well-connected individuals and families in all the eastern Indian groups adapted rather easily to a market-based economy resting on cotton or wheat production. These people instituted cultural modifications such as possession of private property, slave ownership, and constitutional government in accordance with broader American patterns. Nevertheless, Indian groups as a whole remained staunchly resistant to land cessions, negating one of the principal desired effects of "civilization" from the American perspective.

Jefferson Advocates Indian Removal

Although he did not put Indian removal into action, Thomas Jefferson was the first president to advocate the possibility of the scheme. In late 1802 and early 1803, Jefferson wrote several letters and issued official messages that urged the creation of federally run trading posts, with the intention, among other things, of putting Indians into debt. He realized that the fur trade was a dying practice east of the Mississippi River and that Indians would have to pay their debts with land cessions. Jefferson also suggested that any

Many North American Indian groups relied on agriculture for survival and employed people to protect the crops from birds and other pests.

1828

February 16 Ho-Chunk man, Red Bird, dies in American captivity.

December 3 Andrew Jackson is elected president of the United States.

October John Ross becomes principal chief of the Cherokee Nation after the death of the former chief, Path Killer. He leads the legal fight against Indian removal.

December 20 Georgia passes laws extending state jurisdiction over all Indian lands within their borders, sparking a constitutional crisis with the U.S. government.

1828–1829

The Yokut uprising occurs against Mexican forces in central California.

1828–1835

The Cherokee Nation publishes a newspaper, the *Phoenix*, in both English and the Cherokee syllabary invented by Sequoya.

1829

The American Fur Company establishes the Fort Union trading post at the mouth of the Yellowstone River.

Pequot man William Apess publishes *A Son of the Forest: The Experience of William Apess, a Native of the Forest.*

1829–1851

Treaties between the United States and the Winnebago, Chippewa (Ojibway), Eastern Sioux, and Menominee tribes calls for their removal west of the Mississippi River.

Indian group "foolhardy enough to take up the hatchet" against the United States would be driven from the East. He further added that Indians "will in time either incorporate with us as citizens of the United States or remove beyond the Mississippi." Jefferson negotiated the 1803 Louisiana Purchase, securing American-owned land to which eastern Indians could be banished.

Economic, demographic, racist, and local pressures for Indian removal increased in the early nineteenth century. Eli Whitney's cotton gin, perfected in 1793, enabled the efficient processing of short-staple cotton that grew well throughout the interior South. As a result, Euro-American settlers relocated to the Mississippi Territory, established in 1798 and encompassing present-day Mississippi and Alabama, to cultivate cotton. These newcomers began to demand access to Choctaw, Chickasaw, Creek, and Cherokee lands in those areas. In Georgia, calls for Cherokee removal reached new heights when gold was discovered on Cherokee lands in the late 1820s. In the North, the completion of the Erie Canal in 1825 across the state of New York encouraged Euro-American emigration to the west and dramatically increased pressures on

Indians from New York to Wisconsin to move westward. The short-lived Black Hawk War in 1832, in which the Sac and Fox Indians fought white settlers in Indiana and Wisconsin, further sharpened northern voices against Indians remaining in the East. The cries of settlers in southern and other western states highlighted another major component of Indian removal: the conflict between states and the federal government over Indian relations and control of land. States demanded control over all lands within their borders, whereas the federal government insisted, per the U.S. constitution, that it alone could negotiate with Indians who maintained a treaty relationship with the United States. Settlers and elected officials in the newer western states grew increasingly strident in their denunciation of Indians, and violence sometimes resulted. No matter how much a particular Indian group became "civilized," they encountered uncompromising racism among Americans, who had adopted a new scientific explanation of racial differences in the early

....

Thomas Jefferson's policy encouraged Indians to trade furs and go into debt that would be paid with land cessions.

1830

Mohican chief Hendrick Aupaumut dies. He had led his people from New England to resettle in Wisconsin.

May 28 U.S. Congress passes the Indian Removal Act, which authorizes the president to negotiate with eastern Indian tribes for their removal west of the Mississippi River.

September 28 The Treaty of Dancing Rabbit Creek is agreed, whereby the Choctaws sign a removal treaty with the United States and start moving to the Indian Territory (later Oklahoma).

1831

March 18 The U.S. Supreme Court case *Cherokee Nation v. Georgia* takes place. The Cherokees sue Georgia for unconstitutionally extending jurisdiction over their lands.

March 18 Chief Justice John Marshall characterizes Indian groups within the United States as "domestic dependent nations."

The cotton gin revolutionized cotton production in the American South.

nineteenth century, which argued that Indians would always remain "savages" no matter their actual accomplishments.

Americans in favor of Indian removal received a boost in 1828 when one of their own, Andrew Jackson, was elected president. After defeating the Red Sticks at the Battle of Horseshoe Bend, Jackson moved his forces southward and defended New Orleans from British attack, earning him national fame. He also led an invasion of Spanish Florida in 1818 against the Seminole and remaining Red Stick Indians, killing several of their chiefs. He captured Spanish Pensacola, and in 1819, when Spain sold Florida to the United States, Jackson was named governor of the Florida Territory. By 1823 he was running for president of the United States. In the 1828 election, Jackson and his Democratic Party won easily, establishing the man made famous as a fighter of Indians as commander in chief of the entire U.S. military. State politicians, especially in the South, responded to his election by passing laws that

1831–1832

Treaties between the United States and the Shawnees, Ottawas, Wyandots, Piankashaws, Weas, Peorias, Kaskaskias, Delawares, Menominees, and Kickapoos call for their removal west of the Mississippi River.

1831–1842

Treaties between the United States and the Senecas, Oneidas, Onondagas, Cayugas, Tuscaroras, Munsees, St. Regis, Stockbridge, and Brotherton call for their removal west of the Mississippi River.

1832

March 3 The U.S. Supreme Court case *Worcester v. Georgia* is heard. The Supreme Court rules that Georgia has no constitutional right to interfere in Cherokee affairs and that state laws do not extend to Indian-owned territory.

May Winnebago and Sauk prophet White Cloud encourages Black Hawk to fight the Americans by prophesying that the British and other Indian groups would aid the fight.

March 4 A treaty with the Creeks calls for them to relinquish their communal land titles and promotes their removal west of the Mississippi River.

May Sauk war chief Black Hawk leads the armed resistance against the American presence on his people's ancestral lands in Illinois and Wisconsin.

May 10 The Black Hawk War is fought in Illinois and Wisconsin. Militant Indian resistance east of the Mississippi River ends with this conflict.

October 20 The Pontotoc Creek Treaty with the Chickasaws calls for their removal west of the Mississippi River.

extended state jurisdiction over Indian lands. Georgia was the first to do so on December 20, 1828, extending state jurisdiction over Cherokee lands in northwestern Georgia, but delaying enforcement until June 1830 in order to give Jackson and the federal government time to support their action. Alabama passed a law extending its jurisdiction over Creek Indian lands in January 1829. Mississippi passed a resolution claiming jurisdiction over Choctaw and Chickasaw lands within its borders, and this was signed into law by the governor on February 4, 1829. Therefore, southern states enabled Jackson to mask Indian removal as a solution to the conflict between the rights of states and federal jurisdiction and power.

The Indian Removal Act

After much debate and a close vote in Congress, President Jackson signed the Indian Removal Act into law on May 29, 1830. The act called on the president to negotiate removal treaties with Indian groups and to exchange lands west

The Erie Canal in New York connected Albany with Buffalo in the 1820s, bringing settlers into the upper Midwest.

1832–1836

Treaties between the United States and the Potawatomis calls for their removal west of the Mississippi River.

1833

German Prince Maximilian and Swiss artist Karl Bodmer travel up the Missouri River, collecting artifacts and painting images of northern Plains Indians.

Chickasaw removal begins in northern Mississippi.

Potawatomi removals begin in Illinois and Indiana.

Creek removal begins in Alabama.

1833–1841

Treaties with the Miamis call for their removal west of the Mississippi River.

of the Mississippi River for Indian lands in the east. In his State of the Union speech that December, Jackson applauded the act on humanitarian terms, stating that removal at federal government expense provided Indians with a chance of survival and demonstrated the "humanity and national honor" of the United States in taking action to save "these people." Despite Jackson's generous line of reasoning in support of Indian removal, the Indian Removal Act forced Indians to choose between removal and retaining some autonomy or being subject entirely to the laws of the state where they resided. Choctaws were the first Indian group to be moved west, after signing the Treaty of Dancing Rabbit Creek in the late summer of 1830. The first few thousand Choctaws left for the Indian Territory that winter, and hundreds died. Indians responded to the call for removal in a variety of ways. Some individuals accepted the seeming inevitability of removal and negotiated treaties to their best possible advantage, while others refused to accept

Andrew Jackson at the Battle of New Orleans. Jackson became president and implemented Indian removal.

1834

The American Fur Company builds the Fort Laramie trading post on the Platte River.

1835

December 29 The Treaty of New Echota is agreed, in which an unauthorized group of Cherokees called the "treaty party" signs a removal treaty with the United States.

1835–1842

Seminole chief Osceola leads the Seminoles in resisting American expansion in Florida.

The Second Seminole War breaks out when the Seminoles refuse to abide by treaties made in 1832 and 1833 that call for their removal west of the Mississippi River.

removal by fighting back legally as well as physically, staying in their homelands or moving somewhere other than the Indian Territory. The impact of the removal treaties was as dramatic as any other episode in the long history of relations between Indians and Euro-Americans, and continues to shape Indian affairs throughout the United States today.

Cherokee Resistance

No Indian group more vigorously opposed Indian removal than the Cherokees. As pressures mounted to move west of the Mississippi, Cherokees used U.S. law to try to hold on to their lands. The most effective Cherokee voice against the removal policy belonged to John Ross, the principal chief of the Cherokee Nation. Born in 1790 to a Scottish father and a part-Cherokee mother, Ross became an elite farmer who owned African slaves and grew cotton for sale on the market. Ross and his followers took the Georgia government to court to prevent extension of

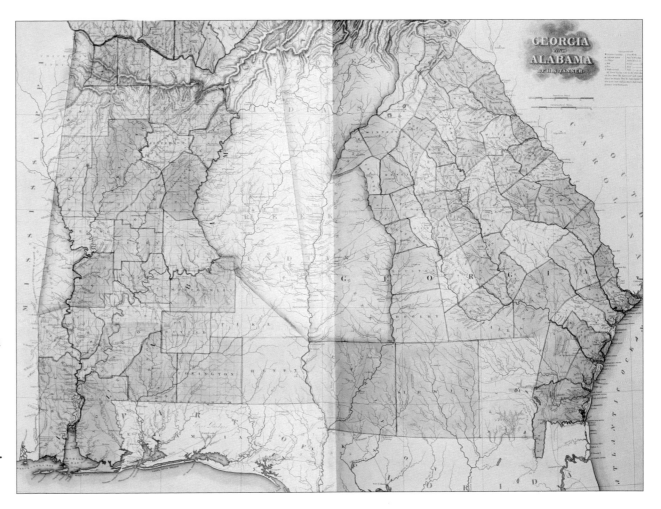

A map of Georgia and Alabama in 1823, showing Creek Indian lands to be relinquished during Indian removal.

1836

February 18 Seneca chief Cornplanter dies.

March 2 Texas becomes independent from Mexico.

The "treaty party" Cherokees leave for the Indian Territory, although most Cherokees did not leave until forced to do so in 1838.

Cherokee chief John Ross denounces the New Echota Treaty and unsuccessfully calls on the U.S. Senate not to approve it.

The ownership of Thomas Selkirk's Red River settlement reverts to the Hudson's Bay Company.

Remaining Creek Indians in Alabama are forcibly moved to the Indian Territory.

1837

July 29 The Pine Tree Treaty is ratified between the United States and the Chippewas. Millions of acres in Wisconsin and Minnesota are ceded to the United States.

October 20 Osceola is captured by U.S. troops after being invited to a peace council and then arrested. He dies in captivity within a year.

state law over their territory. Many Cherokees, such as Ross, had adopted the American system of agriculture and government, owned African slaves, and had vast holdings of crops, horses, cattle, pigs, and other valuable resources.

However, such expressions of "civilization" ironically made them more vulnerable to removal because Americans wanted their productive land. In addition, the Cherokee Nation published its own bilingual newspaper, the *Cherokee Phoenix*; the alphabet for written Cherokee was developed by a Cherokee man named Sequoya. The Cherokee Nation also adopted its own constitution in 1827, based on the U.S. Constitution. The Cherokee constitution made land sales in the Cherokee Nation illegal. There were pressures and splits between elites (progressives) and traditionalists (conservatives), and a rising middle class who were not traditional but had not yet succeeded economically. It was middle-class Cherokees who most supported Indian removal in order to improve their economic condition and position. Ross pulled his base of support from the

Left: *John Ross (1790–1866), principal chief of the Cherokee Nation.*

Right: *A front page from the* Cherokee Phoenix, *published in both Cherokee and English.*

1837–1840

1837–1838 A smallpox epidemic decimates Indian populations on the northern plains and along the Missouri River, especially among the Mandans, Hidatsas, and Arikaras.

1837–1840 Remaining Chickasaws in northern Mississippi are forcibly moved to the Indian Territory, where they reside on Choctaw lands.

1838

October 3 Sauk war chief Black Hawk dies among his people who lived in exile in Iowa.

1838–1840

Remaining eastern Cherokees are forcibly moved to the Indian Territory over the "Trail of Tears."

Some eastern Cherokees led by Yonaguska remain in southwestern North Carolina on private land, where their descendants exist today as the Eastern Band of Cherokees.

1840

The Cheyennes and Arapahos make peace with the Comanches, Kiowas, and plains Apaches.

Francis Godfroy, a Miami Indian trader and advocate for Miami sovereignty in Indiana, dies.

conservative Cherokees who avoided acculturation to American ways.

In 1830 after the passage of the Indian Removal Act, the Cherokee Nation sued Georgia in the U.S. Supreme Court, asking for an injunction to prevent Georgia's seizure of Cherokee lands. Attorneys for the Cherokees argued that, as an independent nation, the Cherokees could not be subject to state jurisdiction. Chief Justice John Marshall sympathized with the Cherokee position, but declined to issue an injunction against Georgia because Indian nations in the United States were "domestic dependent nations" rather than independent foreign nations and their relationship to the United States "resembles that of a ward to his guardian," and he therefore disqualified them from suing in the Supreme Court.

The Cherokees had gained some sympathy for their plight across the United States, and they eagerly pursued another chance to bring the issue of their sovereignty to the Supreme Court. From March 1831, Georgia required any white person living in Cherokee country to have a license issued by the state. Missionaries Samuel Worcester and Elizur Butler ignored this

condition, then were subsequently arrested by Georgian authorities, and later appealed their case to the Supreme Court. In that case, *Worcester v. Georgia* (1832), Marshall declared Georgia's extension of state law over the Cherokees' unconstitutional law and ordered the release of the missionaries. Georgia refused to abide by the decision and the executive branch of the federal government declined to compel Georgia's compliance. The Cherokees won their legal battle, but Georgia's refusal to honor that decision nullified their victory.

After 1832, Cherokees became less united in their determination to hold on to their lands. A significant minority, called the "treaty party," worked to get a removal treaty signed by the U.S. government. A group of these men signed a removal treaty with Secretary of War John Eaton in Washington, D.C., and Jackson submitted it to the Senate in June 1834. The Senate, however, tabled the treaty, refusing to discuss it. Aware that there existed a group among the Cherokees willing to sign a removal

treaty, the Jackson administration sent a representative to the Cherokee Nation in February 1835 to negotiate with them. The treaty party was dominated by four related men who aspired to elite status: Major Ridge, his

The Cherokee alphabet devised by the Cherokee man Sequoya and learned by Cherokees in the 1820s.

1842

Seneca Indians are moved to the Allegheny and Cattaraugus reservations in New York.

1845

Some Seminoles migrate to Mexico to escape American contact.

1846–1848

War between the United States and Mexico results in the American acquisition of Texas, New Mexico, Arizona, Colorado, Nevada, and California.

May Miami Indians are moved from Indiana to the Indian Territory.

1846–1868

A protracted war is waged between the United States and various Apache groups in the Southwest.

Apache warriors Mangas Coloradas and Cochise lead resistance against the United States.

educated son John Ridge, and his two nephews, the brothers Elias Boudinot and Stand Watie. Opposing them were the majority of Cherokees united under principal chief John Ross's leadership. Ridge and his relatives signed a removal treaty on March 14, 1835, but this was rejected by the Cherokee council and therefore nullified. In December 1835, another meeting with U.S. negotiators was held at New Echota, with only Ridge's supporters bothering to attend, and a removal treaty was signed on December 29. The Cherokee council condemned the treaty and Ross appealed to the U.S. Senate to reject it, but the Senate approved it by a one-vote margin. The treaty party Cherokees emigrated to the Indian Territory immediately, while the treaty required the rest of the eastern Cherokees to leave by May 12, 1838. Ross and 15,000 Cherokees who opposed the treaty appealed repeatedly to have the Treaty of New Echota voided, but they encountered little sympathy from the U.S. government. General Winfield Scott arrived in the Cherokee country

···

John Marshall (1755–1835), Chief Justice of the U.S. Supreme Court, who supported Cherokee sovereignty.

in the summer of 1838 to oversee the forced relocation of the Cherokees, which resulted in numerous deaths along the Trail of Tears and the loss of property at the hands of rapacious whites. The split among the Cherokees continued after removal because Cherokees who opposed removal killed Major Ridge, John Ridge, and Elias Boudinot. Watie and Ross competed for political power from the late 1830s until the Civil War in the 1860s. Some Cherokees were able to hole up in western North Carolina, where their descendants have a reservation today.

Indians on the Plains

To Plains Indians—as contemporary citizens of the United States and Canada usually know them—the riding of horses, the hunting of buffalo with rifles, and the wearing of headdresses was a phenomenon that existed only in the eighteenth and nineteenth centuries. Europeans—and the animals and technology they brought with them—greatly altered Plains Indian culture and gave rise to the stereotypical Indian that existed in the nineteenth century as the United States and Canada expanded

---

1847

January 19 The Taos pueblo in New Mexico revolts against U.S. authority.

1848

Gold discovered in California results in massive American migration to the area and a sharp decline in Californian Indian populations.

1849

Fort Laramie is purchased by the U.S. government and converted to a military fort.

March 3 U.S. Indian service is transferred from the War Department to the Department of the Interior.

1849–1850

At the Pomo Indian massacre in California, 130 men, women, and children are killed by American soldiers.

A cholera epidemic sweeps the Great Plains.

1849–1854

A British colony is established on Vancouver Island. The Hudson's Bay Company negotiates fourteen treaties with First Nations groups.

westward. Even before Europeans arrived in North America, the Plains Indians were undergoing constant change with shifts in the balance of power and the movement of groups onto the plains. Two types of Plains peoples greeted Euro-Americans: horticultural people who lived along the river valleys, such as the Caddos, Wichitas, Pawnees, Arikaras, Mandans, Hidatsas, Missouris, Otos, Iowas, Omahas, Poncas, Kansas, and Osages; and nomadic people who relied solely on hunting buffalo for subsistence, such as the Kiowas, Lakota Sioux, Cheyennes, Blackfeet, Crees, Gros Ventres, Arapahos, Assiniboines, Crows, Comanches, and Shoshones.

Stand Watie was a chief political rival of John Ross, and supported the Confederacy in the U.S. Civil War.

Guns and horses severely impacted tribal relations and politics on the plains. They spread when nomadic tribes of the plains traded with more settled horticultural peoples at annual summertime trade gatherings. Guns came in the seventeenth and eighteenth centuries from the Northeast (Great Lakes) and the Southeast through French posts in Louisiana. Horses came from the South via Mexico and New Mexico. Buffalo, which attracted new tribes to the plains, experienced a great increase in numbers around 1600 due to the end of a long series of droughts; there were at least 30 million— and probably closer to 60 million—buffalo on the plains when Europeans began to contact the region. Owning guns and horses, combined with access to

A Mandan Indian village on the upper Missouri River like ones seen by the Lewis and Clark expedition in 1804.

buffalo, meant increased power and prosperity for many Plains Indian groups. With horses and guns, buffalo hunting was made easier and was often more productive than farming. Indian groups fought with each other over access to prime hunting grounds, and many that had never hunted buffalo began to do so.

Tribes without guns and horses, who fought against other Indians who possessed the new technology, were doomed to defeat. In 1730, for example, the Blackfeet from the northern plains prepared to fight the Shoshones from the

1850

Britain negotiates the Robinson Treaties with Native peoples on the north shores of Lake Huron and Lake Superior.

1851

September 17 The first Treaty of Fort Laramie between the United States and several Plains Indian groups establishes tribal boundaries.

1852

Quechan Indians of southern Arizona rebel against Americans constructing Fort Yuma on their lands.

1853

The Walker War ends when Mormon leader Brigham Young and Ute leader Walkara meet and negotiate an end to hostilities.

July 17 The Walker War breaks out between Utes and Mormon colonists in Utah.

1853–1855

The Rogue River Indian War is waged in Oregon between various bands of Indians against the U.S. Army and local American colonists over access to natural resources.

southwestern plains in traditional combat, but the Shoshones had guns and horses. The Shoshones routed the Blackfeet and pushed them north into Canada. By the late eighteenth century, however, the Blackfeet had retaliated with their own guns and horses, driving the Shoshones back to the South. The Blackfeet then prevented Europeans and Americans from trading guns to tribes to their west in order to prevent their enemies from gaining the same advantage. By 1800 the Blackfeet grew to be the major military power in the northwestern plains. Such new dominance remained fleeting; the Blackfeet suffered major smallpox epidemics in 1837 and 1869. Other Indian groups, especially the Lakota Sioux, moved in to take the place of the Blackfeet as the strongest Indian military power.

The Comanches also moved onto the plains from the Rocky Mountains. The Comanches originated in southwestern Wyoming and are culturally related to the eastern Shoshones. From the seventeenth century, they pushed

An Assiniboine village showing Indian adoption of the horse, after its introduction to North America.

1854

August 19 The Grattan Massacre precipitates the U.S. Army's expedition against the Lakota Sioux in the Platte River country.

1855

The Choctaws agree to sell the western portion of their Indian Territory lands to the Chickasaws, reestablishing Chickasaw sovereignty.

1855–1858

The Third Seminole War in Florida results in stalemate as the U.S. Army could not locate or defeat Seminole forces that retreated to the Everglades swamps.

Seminole chief Billy Bowlegs leads resistance to the United States after the Americans destroy his crops.

The Yakima War is fought in the Northwest between the Yakama Indians and other Native groups against newly arrived American colonists.

1858

September 1 The U.S. Army defeats Yakama Indian forces at the Battle of Four Lakes near Spokane and force the Indians to live on reservations.

The Fraser River gold rush occurs. Prospectors establish a colony on the mainland of British Columbia, and conflicts develop between Native people and gold seekers.

southward on to the southern plains into New Mexico and across to Texas. By 1800 the Comanches controlled the southern plains, and were the largest and most powerful group in all the plains except for the Lakota Sioux to the north. As they acquired guns and horses, they changed much of their culture to center around horses, buffalo, and warfare. These changes included a deterioration in the status of women as the Comanches abandoned farming and warfare became the norm. In 1840 the Comanches and the Kiowas (who had been pushed to the south from the Black Hills by the Lakota Sioux) concluded a peace with the Cheyennes, Arapahos, and Kiowa-Apaches in the southern plains to unite against both Texans and tribes from the east who had been removed to the Indian Territory. The intention was to save buffalo population numbers and their relatively new way of life.

Buffalo

The buffalo population on the plains began to decrease from their peak even before American hunters had arrived in the area in significant numbers in the nineteenth century. As with the

Indians hunting buffalo in the nineteenth century with guns and horses.

deer and beaver fur trades that had dominated Indian-European relations earlier, Plains Indians hunted buffalo not only for their own consumption but also for trade with Americans. Another reason for the decline in buffalo was the horses that Plains Indians had adopted to make buffalo hunting easier. Horses ate the

same food as buffalo and, with approximately 2 million wild horses and half a million domesticated horses on the plains by the nineteenth century, the competition over grasses resulted in fewer buffalo. Decreasing buffalo numbers meant more violence between Indian groups and competition for control over

1859–1864

Navajos rebel against the United States at Fort Defiance, Arizona.

Navajo chief Manuelito organizes the Navajo resistance to the United States after American soldiers kill his livestock.

1861–1865

The Civil War is fought. Indian groups, especially in the Indian Territory, assist both Union and Confederate forces according to their perceived best interests.

Cherokee man Stand Watie gains fame as a cavalry leader and Confederate general.

Choctaw cavalry leader Tandy Walker gains fame as an effective ally of the Confederacy.

territories still rich in resources. It was at this time, in the early to mid-nineteenth century, that the United States entered the plains and recognized that Plains Indian tribes emphasized martial skills to a higher degree than most other Native tribes on the continent. The Americans generally failed to recognize the historically contingent nature of this warrior culture and attributed the Plains Indians' skill in war to their "savage" nature. The Indians who seemed to benefit most from the new trade realities of buffalo, guns, and horses—and who captivated the American imagination in the nineteenth century and since—were the Lakota Sioux.

Lakota Sioux

Originally from the western Great Lakes and Minnesota area, the Lakotas acquired some horses and guns as early as 1700 but did not incorporate them as a defining element of their culture until the mid-eighteenth century. At that point, they abandoned their horticultural, beaver-hunting lifestyle for buffalo hunting on the plains. Made up of the Oglala, Hunkpapa, Miniconjou, Brulé, Blackfoot (Sihaspa), Sans Arc, and Two Kettles bands, the Lakotas

Plains Indians returning from war with a combination of traditional weapons and newer firearms and horses.

expanded onto the plains and pushed other tribes out of the way. They developed the quintessential Plains Indian warrior culture that depended on horses, guns, and hunting buffalo. By the time of the Lewis and Clark expedition in 1804–06, the Lakota Sioux had become the dominant power in the northern plains and on the upper Missouri River.

Lakota relations with the United States tell the story of American expansion into the plains and Indian resistance. The Lakotas never accepted the terms of the first treaty with the United States, the Treaty of Fort Laramie in 1851. This persuaded the Lakotas, Crows, Cheyennes, Arapahos, Assiniboines, Gros Ventres, and Arrikaras to set boundaries between themselves and other tribes. The United States claimed the right to establish roads and military posts within Indian territories, promising to pay annuities. The U.S. government also tampered with Indian culture by recognizing "head chiefs," who were expected to control their respective peoples, and by distributing agricultural implements such as hoes. This treaty did not establish reservations but, by establishing boundaries between tribes

1862

March 7 The Battle of Pea Ridge in Arkansas includes 800 Cherokee Confederate soldiers.

Smallpox epidemics sweep through British Columbia, killing a third of the Native population in the Canadian province.

1862–1864

Santee Sioux in Minnesota rebel against the unfair and corrupt practices of the U.S. Indian agent, which have resulted in starvation of Santee people.

Approximately 1,300 Kickapoos from Kansas migrate southward to Mexico to escape violence from Americans.

Santee Sioux leader Little Crow organizes the uprising against whites in Minnesota.

1863

July 3 Santee Sioux leader Little Crow is executed, along with thirty-seven other Santee warriors, by the U.S. government.

Seminole leader Billy Bowlegs dies.

Karl Bodmer's Scalp Dance of the Minatarres, *c. 1840. Bodmer traveled up the Missouri River in the early 1830s as part of Prince Maximilian zu Wied's exploring party.*

1863–1864

U.S. forces under Kit Carson round up 8,000 Navajos and force them to march 350 miles on the Long Walk to confinement at the Bosque Redondo.

1863–1867

Lakota Sioux chief Red Cloud leads the military effort to close the Bozeman Trail in Montana.

1864

October 14 Cheyenne chief Black Kettle survives the Sand Creek Massacre and leads his followers to western Oklahoma to live on a reservation.

October 14 The Klamath Reservation in southern Oregon is established by a treaty between the United States and the Klamath, Modoc, and Yahooskin tribes.

November 29 At the Sand Creek Massacre in Colorado, militia volunteers murder hundreds of Cheyennes and Arapahos.

1864–1872

During the Lowry War in North Carolina, Lumbees insist on civil rights and identity as Native people.

Fort Laramie, Wyoming Territory, where U.S. representatives negotiated a treaty in 1851 with nearly a dozen northern Plains Indian groups.

that could be shrunk over time, it set the stage for confining western Indians. The Lakotas disagreed with the territory limits in the treaty because they had conquered the Crows from eastern Montana and the Kiowas from the Black Hills but were now being told to give up some of those lands.

Direct conflicts with Americans began in 1854, when a Lakota warrior killed a nearly dead ox belonging to a Mormon wagon train. The Lakotas offered payment for the ox, but the Mormons and Second Lieutenant John Grattan at Fort Laramie refused. Grattan and a force of thirty cavalry tried to arrest the Lakota chief, Conquering Bear, but killed him instead. His warriors then destroyed Grattan's forces except for one man, and plundered posts and stages along the Platte River to Fort Laramie. The next year, Colonel William Harney and 1,300 troops were sent to subdue the Lakotas, but they attacked the Sioux who had played no part in the Grattan battles, killing eighty-six men, women, and children. For the Sioux, such loss was unprecedented: traditionally the deaths of as few as ten men in a battle represented catastrophe.

1865

Cheyennes, Arapahos, and Lakotas raid Americans up and down the North Platte and South Platte rivers.

1865–1872

The Black Hawk War is waged in Utah between Mormon colonists and members of the Ute, Paiute, and Navajo tribes.

Ute chief Black Hawk leads the fighting against Mormons in Utah.

1866

Lakota war leader Crazy Horse organizes the defeat of Capain William Fetterman's forces.

December 21 Lakota forces defeat the U.S. Army cavalry unit in the Fetterman Massacre as part of Lakota efforts to close the Bozeman Trail in Montana.

1867

March 29 Canada is created under the terms of the British North America Act.

October 18 The United States purchases Alaska from Russia, bringing the government into contact with the dozens of Indian peoples there.

October The Treaty of Medicine Lodge Creek is ratified between the United States and southern Plains groups such as the Kiowas, Comanches, Cheyennes, Plains Apaches, and Arapahos.

In 1856 the U.S. Army conducted its first large-scale exploration of the Black Hills, an area sacred to the Lakotas and many other Plains Indian groups. In 1857 all seven of the Lakota Sioux tribes met in the summer in the Black Hills and pledged never to cede any of those lands. In 1858 the U.S. government convinced the Yankton Sioux to sell the eastern Dakotas, an area of nearly 15 million acres, and white settlers began to migrate to the region in large numbers. In 1859 the discovery of gold in Colorado launched an American exodus across the plains, with 80,000 Americans living in Colorado by 1862. Buffalo fled to the north and south—away from the roads and trails used by the Americans; the Lakotas claimed that if a buffalo even smelled a white man, it fled. In 1861 Montana became the latest area where gold was discovered, bringing miners and prospectors into the heart of Lakota and other northern Plains Indian homelands, and setting the stage for further conflict.

The U.S. Civil War in Indian Country

As with the colonial wars for empire of a century before, American Indians fought on both sides of

Douglas H. Cooper (1815–1879) served as U.S. agent to the Choctaws and Chickasaws in the Indian Territory.

this conflict and suffered greatly from the violence and the scarcity of supplies. The war was very destructive in the Indian Territory, where many tribes had been banished earlier in the nineteenth century. Among the five major southeastern Indian groups—the Choctaws, Chickasaws, Creeks, Seminoles, and Cherokees—war between Confederate and Union factions erupted. The five southeastern groups maintained strong ties with the Southern states and, despite Southern involvement in their removal to the West, they generally viewed the U.S. government with bitterness. The U.S. Indian agents in the Indian Territory at the start of the war came from the South, such as Douglas Cooper of Mississippi, agent to the Choctaws and Chickasaws. Supporting his home state's secessionist stance, Cooper worked on his Indian charges to do the same. Elites among the five southeastern groups maintained trade and transportation ties with the Southern states and also owned African slaves and planted cotton. In early 1861, as war loomed, the federal government removed troops from the Indian Territory, enabling Confederate agents to persuade the southeastern Indians to ally with the Confederacy.

1867–1870

Osages, Pawnees, Shawnees, Delawares, and Oto-Missouris resettle in the Indian Territory.

1868

April 29 The second Treaty of Fort Laramie is signed. The United States acknowledges defeat by Red Cloud's Lakota forces and establishes the Great Sioux Reservation.

June 1 The Treaty of Bosque Redondo establishes the Navajo Reservation in Arizona and New Mexico, and Navajos return to the Four Corners region of the Southwest.

November 27 At the Battle of the Washita in western Oklahoma, the U.S. Seventh Cavalry under George Armstrong Custer attacks a peaceful Cheyenne village.

November 27 Cheyenne chief Black Kettle is killed by the U.S. Seventh Cavalry.

The Choctaws and Chickasaws signed treaties with the Confederacy with little hesitation, but for other Indian groups in the Indian Territory, the decision did not come easily. The Cherokees, for example, were divided over the war and ended up fighting their own civil war. The primary dispute among the Cherokees was between chief John Ross and Stand Watie, who had been a member of the treaty party that signed the 1835 Treaty of New Echota calling for Cherokee removal. Watie remained opposed to Ross and, under threat of assassination, organized a militia force that surrounded him at all times. Ross and Watie were both very wealthy and owned dozens of slaves, but the Civil War opened up old wounds. Ross's followers (conservatives) generally did not own slaves, whereas Watie's followers (middle-class planters and farmers) were much more likely to engage in a cash-crop agriculture and own slaves. Confederate

Albert Pike convinced a large contingent of the Cherokees in Indian Territory to support the Confederacy in the Civil War.

representative Albert Pike negotiated with the Cherokees in 1861 to join the Confederacy, which was accomplished with Ross's approval in October 1861. The treaties that the Confederacy signed with all of the southeastern nations

promised protection from U.S. troops, offered to pay the same annuities the U.S. government had paid, and allowed Indian representation in the Confederate congress. The Indians had to supply troops to protect the Indian Territory from a Union takeover. Watie had already gained a commission as a colonel in June 1861 and had begun raising troops for the Confederacy. The Cherokees formed two cavalry regiments: one under Watie and another under Ross, led by his nephew John Drew. Watie's men were much more pro-Confederacy and Drew's men defected to the Union after the Battle of Pea Ridge in March 1862. Ross and the conservatives moved north to Unionist Kansas, renounced their treaty with the Confederacy, and abolished slavery by 1863. This change of heart left Watie, who became a Confederate brigadier general, in control of the Cherokee Nation in the Indian Territory. Watie's forces fought several winning battles against Unionist Creeks and Cherokees. Watie and his men won a number of small battles using guerrilla tactics and did not surrender until June 23, 1865, making Waite the last Confederate general to do so. Pro-Confederate Chickasaw and Caddo

1869

April 10 U.S. President Ulysses S. Grant creates the Board of Indian commissioners.

April 21 Seneca man Ely S. Parker becomes the first Indian to head the Bureau of Indian Affairs.

1869–1870

The Red River Rebellion in Manitoba, Canada, erupts after the new dominion of Canada purchases former Hudson's Bay Company land in Manitoba.

Métis man Louis Riel leads the Red River Rebellion that results in the creation of Manitoba, Canada, as a separate province.

President Grant's peace policy seeks to end wars against Indians in the West and reform the Indian service.

A smallpox epidemic hits the northern plains.

forces officially surrendered on July 14, 1865, the last major Confederate forces to give up.

After the war, the Cherokee Nation and all of the Indian Territory lay in ruins with thousands of people dead or living as refugees, livestock dead, crops and fields destroyed, and houses and other buildings burned to the ground. As many as 10,000 Indian people died in Indian Territory during the war. Anarchy prevailed everywhere, with gangs of outlaws robbing and killing. Even though significant portions of the southeastern Indian groups remained pro-Union, the U.S. government forced all of them to relinquish some land in the Indian Territory.

Post–Civil War U.S.-Indian Relations

The Civil War did not stop American migration to the West. In 1862 the Santee Sioux, led principally by a chief named Little Crow, rebelled against American settlers in Minnesota. Many Santee Sioux were starving and were not receiving the provisions that had been promised in their treaties with the United States. They killed more than 700 whites before the U.S. Army killed or captured hundreds of Santees and sentenced more than 300 of them to death.

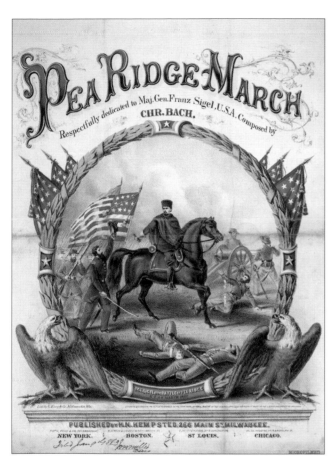

Union General Franz Sigel at the Battle of Pea Ridge in Arkansas on March 8, 1862.

Santee Sioux leader Little Crow, who led the Indian uprising in Minnesota against American settlers in 1862.

1870

The United States forces Arikara, Gros Ventre, and Mandan Indians to live on the Fort Berthold Reservation in the Dakota Territory.

May 12 Creation of the Manitoba Province in Canada and the protection of Métis and Native land title in the area.

1871

May 1 The Cherokee Tobacco Case extends federal tax law to Indian nations.

U.S. Congress ends the practice of making treaties with American Indians.

1871–1875

The first five numbered treaties between the new government of Canada and Native peoples result in large land cessions in areas of Manitoba and the Northwest Territories.

1871–1879

The U.S. government sponsors the wholesale slaughter of buffalo herds on the plains as a strategy to force Plains Indians to live on reservations.

President Lincoln commuted most of the sentences, although thirty-eight were hanged in Mankato, Minnesota, the largest mass execution in U.S. history. Many surviving Santees fled west to live with their Lakota relatives and continue the fight. In 1864, in the context of the Santee revolt, feelings ran high among Americans. Militia colonel John Chivington, with volunteers from the streets of Denver, attacked and massacred Black Kettle's peaceful Cheyenne band at Sand Creek in eastern Colorado, mutilating the bodies and displaying body parts in Denver.

Meanwhile, tensions between Lakotas and Americans increased. In 1865 Americans began surveying and building trails, such as the Bozeman Trail from Fort Laramie to Montana, with a goal of making travel easier to the gold fields. The Oglala chief, Red Cloud, led Lakotas in opposing this intrusion. From 1866 to 1867, Red Cloud fought against the U.S. Army as it built posts in Montana to protect the trail. The Lakotas won this war in overwhelming fashion.

The Fetterman Massacre on December 21, 1866, a victory for Lakota forces under Crazy Horse.

1872

After around 150 battles, with atrocities committed by both sides, the Black Hawk War in Utah ends when U.S. troops arrive in the area.

The Chickasaw Oil and Gas Company is founded.

1872–1873

The Modoc War in California and Oregon is waged. The Modocs clash with the U.S. Army in an attempt to stay on their ancestral lands.

1873

April 11 The Modocs ambush and kill the American Indian commissioner, General Canby, and after several battles are forced to live on the Klamath Reservation.

June 1 Captain Jack is captured by American forces during the Modoc War and executed for killing General Canby.

June 1 The Cypress Hills Massacre occurs in southern Alberta, in which a group of American fur hunters massacre thirty-six innocent Assiniboines.

In one battle on December 21, 1866, known as the Fetterman Massacre, the Lakotas under Red Cloud and the war leader Crazy Horse drew Captain William Fetterman's eighty men into a trap and killed all of them. In the late summer of 1868, George Custer led the Seventh Cavalry against the remnants of Little Thunder's Cheyenne band who had been at the Sand Creek Massacre. In this engagement, called the Battle of the Washita, Custer's troops killed a dozen Cheyenne warriors together with ninety women, children, and old men. The Cheyennes were allies of the Lakota Sioux, and the Lakotas drew the lesson that

....

Left: Oglala Lakota chief Red Cloud, c. 1915, who led Lakota warriors against the U.S. Army.

Right: General George Armstrong Custer, pictured here during the Civil War.

this same fate of unrestrained warfare and destruction awaited them too.

In the 1868 Treaty of Fort Laramie, the United States acknowledged that it had lost the war over the Bozeman Trail. The treaty established the Great Sioux Reservation, which included all of western South Dakota (including the Black Hills) as well as the hunting grounds in Montana and Wyoming "as long as buffalo exist in sufficient numbers." No Americans could set foot in hunting territories without Sioux permission, and no further treaties or land cessions were allowed without the signatures of three-quarters of all Lakota adult males. The treaty called for the Lakota Sioux to abandon hunting and begin farming, but most refused because buffalo still existed in sufficient numbers so that farming was not necessary. Crazy Horse and the

1874–1875

The Red River War takes place on the southern plains between the United States and the Comanches, Kiowas, southern Cheyennes, and Arapahos.

Comanche chief Quanah Parker leads Indian forces in the Red River War and is the last leader to surrender in 1875.

1875

After nearly twenty battles, the Comanches, Kiowas, southern Cheyennes, and Arapahos surrender and agree to live on reservations.

Americans flock to the sacred Black Hills on Lakota Indian land in the Dakotas in search of gold.

Lakota chief Red Cloud demands that the Americans abide by the 1868 Treaty of Fort Laramie and leave the Black Hills.

Hunkpapa chief, Sitting Bull, rejected the treaty, and—although the Lakotas had won the war—they would not win the peace.

Soon after the 1868 Treaty of Fort Laramie, Americans trickled into the Black Hills anyway, drawn by rumors of gold. In 1874 Custer led an exploratory force into the Black Hills, and reported back stories about abundant gold. Although the Black Hills belonged to the Lakota Sioux, white Americans sought gold in the area by the thousands. The U.S. government reacted by trying to persuade the Lakotas to agree to a new land cession rather than stopping American emigration. At a meeting with U.S. officials, Crazy Horse sent a message through chief Little Big Man that he "will kill the first chief who speaks for selling the Black Hills." The western Lakota bands under Sitting Bull, Crazy Horse, and others refused even to attend the negotiations, and more progressive chiefs refused to sign the new treaty as well. The U.S. Army issued an ultimatum to these uncooperative chiefs in the middle of winter in 1875 for all the Lakota Sioux to come to the reservation agencies by January 31, 1876. Winter travel and Lakota unwillingness to abide by U.S. demands prevented compliance. Therefore, the U.S. Army took to the field in search of the Lakotas in the spring and summer of 1876.

The Battle of the Little Bighorn

In June 1876, Sitting Bull conducted a sun dance, in which he cut over fifty strips of skin from his arms and had a vision of soldiers without ears falling into the Lakota camp. More than 15,000 Lakota Sioux and Cheyennes had

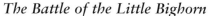

The Battle of the Washita typified the U.S. Army's tactic of attacking Plains Indians in the winter.

1876

Lakotas who refuse to live on reservations, and who are angered by American intrusion into the Black Hills, join forces in Montana.

The Great Sioux War is fought between the U.S. Army and the Lakotas.

October The Indian Act is established in Canada.

Two treaties are negotiated between Canada and Native peoples, especially the Blackfeet, for land cessions and the establishment of Indian reserves.

June 25 General George Armstrong Custer's command is wiped out at the Battle of the Little Bighorn.

A romanticized portrayal of Custer's Last Stand at the Battle of the Little Bighorn on June 25, 1876. Custer's command was routed by Lakota and Cheyenne forces.

1876–1886

War breaks out in the Southwest between the Apaches and the United States. Apache groups, such as the Chiricahuas, refuse to remain confined to reservations.

Chiricahua Apache war leader Geronimo leads the Apaches in resistance to U.S. and Mexican control.

1877

May 6 Lakota war leader and mystic Crazy Horse surrenders at Fort Robinson, Nebraska. He is later murdered by a soldier.

October 5 A Nez Perce man named Chief Joseph leads his people on the arduous 1,400-mile hike in the summer and autumn before surrendering.

Nez Perce Indians in Idaho flee for Canada but are stopped by the U.S. Army just short of the border and forced to surrender.

1878

War breaks out in Idaho between the United States and the Bannocks, Paiutes, and Sheepeaters over access to traditional hunting and gathering lands.

April 14 Kiowa prisoners are sent to the Hampton Institute in Virginia to receive education.

grouped together to hunt buffalo in the summer in defiance of the orders of the U.S. Army. One American force led by General George Crook met 1,500 Cheyenne and Lakota warriors at the Battle of the Rosebud on June 17, 1876. Crook held the field but lost many men and was forced to retreat to his supply post the next morning. This left General Custer and his force of nearly 600 men to fight against the combined Cheyenne, Arapaho, and Lakota encampment. Custer unwisely split his troops into two units and attacked the Indian force on June 25. Sitting Bull, who spent the battle confined to his teepee, saw his vision come true as Custer's men fell into their camp after refusing to listen to the warnings of his Crow Indian scouts, who told him that the Indian force was too big for him to handle without help. More than 260 Americans died, including General Custer, and news of the defeat of the U.S. Army reached the East Coast on July 4, the centennial of the United States. The U.S. government now redoubled its efforts to hunt down the Lakotas and their allies, and within a year all but Sitting Bull's Hunkpapa band, which had fled to Canada, had been attacked and forced to surrender to the reservation agencies.

Louis Riel on trial for treason in Canada in 1885. Riel had led a rebellion of Canadian Métis (French and Native) against the unfair policies of the Canadian government.

1879

Former U.S. Army captain Richard Pratt founds the Carlisle Indian School. According to Pratt, the school sought to "kill the Indian and save the man."

1880

The U.S. government bans the sun dance religious ritual among Plains Indians as part of the effort to force Indians to assimilate into American culture.

1881

January Scholar Helen Hunt Jackson publishes *A Century of Dishonor*, which indicts U.S. Indian policy and the mistreatment of Indian people.

Lakota Sioux leader Sitting Bull brings his people back from exile in Canada to live on the Standing Rock Reservation in the Dakota Territory.

August 5 Brulé Sioux man Crow Dog shoots and kills fellow tribe member Spotted Tail, a pro-assimilation favorite of the U.S. Indian agent on the reservation.

1883

Crow Dog's family pays restitution of $600, eight horses, and a blanket to Spotted Tail's family in order to "cover the dead."

December 17 The U.S. Supreme Court hears the case of *Ex Parte Crow Dog*, which rules that Indian tribes have the right to adjudicate cases involving members of the same tribe.

Sarah Winnemucca, a Paiute woman, publishes *Life Among the Piutes*, an account of her life and Paiute history.

Post–Civil War Canada-Indian Relations

The new independent nation of Canada was created under the terms of the British North America Act of 1867. One of the major priorities of the new government was to extend governing control over western lands. The Red River Rebellion, led by the Métis man Louis Riel, broke out in 1869 in Manitoba, after the new dominion of Canada purchased former Hudson's Bay Company land in Manitoba. Native and Métis people in the area seized Fort Garry and refused to allow Ontario to govern the area. A compromise resulted in the official creation of the Manitoba province and the protection of Métis and Native land titles in the area. From 1871 to 1875, the first five treaties between the new government of Canada and Native peoples were negotiated. Large land cessions resulted in areas that became part of the new province of Manitoba and the Northwest Territories. These are now parts of northwestern Ontario and southern Manitoba, Saskatchewan, and Alberta. In 1876 the Indian Act defined Indian identity, made Indians wards of the Canadian government, created Indian reserves, established Indian boarding schools, and made Indian agents the intermediaries between First Nations people and the rest of the country. From 1876 to 1877, Treaties 6 and 7 were negotiated between Canada and Native peoples, especially the Blackfeet, in southern Saskatchewan and Alberta for land cessions and the establishment of Indian reserves.

The Era of Forced Acculturation

In the nineteenth century, reservations were established by the U.S. government to confine American Indians in areas of land and thus allow most of the West to be opened for American settlement. The era from approximately 1870 to 1920 is often described as the era of forced acculturation, when the goal of the U.S. government was to destroy Indian cultures and turn Indians into "Americans." Reservations were established by treaty, executive order, or congressional decree. Once on reservations, Indians were expected to become farmers, convert to Christianity, and become Americanized through forced schooling. Reservation agents managed the distribution of

Crow Dog, the Brulé Sioux man who killed the pro-assimilationist chief Spotted Tail in 1883.

1884

Anti-potlatch laws are enacted under the Canadian Indian Act. Potlatches are a key component of northwestern First Nations culture and ceremony.

1885

February 10 North Carolina officially recognizes the Croatoan Indians and approves separate schools for their children.

March 3 U.S. Congress passes the Major Crimes Act in response to the 1883 *Ex Parte Crow Dog* decision by the Supreme Court.

Indian police units are established by the U.S. government on forty-eight out of sixty Indian reservations.

November 16 Métis man Louis Riel foments a rebellion in Saskatchewan, resulting in his execution by the Canadian government.

Sitting Bull travels with Buffalo Bill Cody's Wild West Show.

Indian reservations, the allotted land was too small, too arid, or too mountainous to support productive farming. Moreover, the era of successful small farmers was nearing its end as America embraced industry. Although not all Indian reservations suffered through the Allotment Act, many show the scars of that era today with settlement patterns of Indian land interspersed with white-owned land.

Boarding Schools

One of the primary tools employed by the U.S. government to assimilate reservation Indians into American society was boarding schools. The first boarding school established especially to educate Indian children was the Carlisle Indian School, opened by former army officer Richard Pratt in Carlisle, Pennsylvania, in 1879. Within a decade, dozens of similar boarding schools sprang up throughout the country on reservations and in cities. Separated from their parents, Indian children at the schools could not wear traditional clothing, speak their native language, or practice

The mass grave of Wounded Knee Lakota Indian victims, killed on December 29, 1890.

1890

May 2 In the Organic Act, Congress creates the Oklahoma Territory out of the western half of the Indian Territory.

December 29 At the Wounded Knee Massacre, U.S. troops open fire on unarmed Lakota men, women, and children, killing about 300 Lakotas.

The Indian population in the United States reaches an all-time low of less than 250,000.

December 15 Indian police sent to arrest Sitting Bull, the renowned Lakota chief, kill him as he tries to surrender.

December 29 Miniconjou Sioux leader Big Foot dies in the massacre at Wounded Knee.

1891

Dakota man Charles Eastman is stationed at the Pine Ridge Reservation during the Wounded Knee Massacre and writes about the horrors he saw.

January 7 In the aftermath of the Wounded Knee Massacre, a Lakota man, Plenty Horses, kills U.S. Army lieutenant Edward Casey on the Pine Ridge Reservation.

traditional religions. The schools trained Indian students for clerical positions or manual labor such as farming and domestic service. Such skills did little, in most cases, to make these students economically self-sufficient as adults. On the other hand, many Indian students used their new skills in English, math, reading, and writing in productive and fulfilling careers that often enabled them to leave the reservation.

Ghost Dance and Wounded Knee

For American Indians, the nineteenth century ended in a manner similar to the way it began. A major new spiritual revitalization movement began in the mid-1880s under the teachings of Wovoka, a Paiute prophet. Wovoka's message of renewal and communication with dead ancestors, and his new rituals, including dances meant to instigate visions, became popular throughout the plains and Great Basin of North America. Several Indian groups, including the Lakota Sioux on reservations in the Dakotas, transformed Wovoka's spiritual message into one of militant resistance to American ways and American control. For them, Wovoka's message meant the imminent return of the buffalo and the disappearance of the whites. U.S. reservation agents became nervous as the Ghost Dance spread through the West, and they called in the army to round up and keep watch over Indians performing it. Custer's old unit, the Seventh Cavalry, showed up on the Pine Ridge Reservation in December to round up Chief Big Foot's Miniconjou band and bring them to the reservation agency. On December 29, 1890, the Seventh Cavalry massacred Big Foot and about 300 of his people as they tried to disarm them. This disaster is often called the last battle of the Indian wars, and it served mainly to drive home the point that the United States would enforce its will on Indian people with violence whenever it wished to do so.

A segment of the U.S. cavalry leaving Wounded Knee in January 1891.

1893

September 16 The Cherokee Outlet lands in northwestern Oklahoma open for white settlement.

1896

May 18 The U.S. Supreme Court hears *Talton v. Mayes*, and rules that Indian jurisdiction and power antedate the U.S. Constitution.

1898

June 28 U.S. Congress passes the Curtis Act, extending allotment to the Indian Territory and abolishing tribal jurisdiction over lands in the Indian Territory.

July 7 The United States annexes Hawaii as a territory.

1899

The buffalo population declines from several million at the beginning of the nineteenth century to just a few hundred by the end of the century.

1900 to Today

Twentieth-century Native American history is characterized by changing government policies and growing Indian activism. Threats to Indian ownership of land from the U.S. and Canadian governments and corporations continued, but Indians fought the loss of their lands.

In the last decade of the nineteenth century, U.S. Congress began making so-called unassigned lands in the Indian Territory open to American settlement. In 1890 Congress authorized the Jerome Commissions to negotiate allotment agreements with eleven tribes in the western Indian Territory, opening up 15 million acres to American settlement and ranching outfits. Beginning in 1893, hundreds of

Left: Oglala Lakotas on the Pine Ridge Reservation in South Dakota performing the grand entry into a pow-wow, indicative of the persistence of traditional rituals. Right: U.S. Senator Henry Dawes, who supported the Dawes Allotment Act in 1887.

thousands of non-Indians flooded into the western areas, now renamed the Oklahoma Territory. In 1897 Congress sent retired Senator Henry Dawes to the Indian Territory to negotiate allotment agreements with the former southeastern tribes. Railroad and oil companies clamored for access to Indian land and the resources on or underneath the ground. The breaking up of communally held Indian land through allotment was accomplished with the Choctaws and Chickasaws in 1897, the Seminoles in 1898, the Creeks in 1901, and the Cherokees in 1902. In addition, the 1898 Curtis Act called for the dissolution of tribal governments in the Indian Territory. By 1907

the Dawes Commission had completed its work of enrolling Indian people and allotting them land by assigning 19.5 million acres to 101,000 Indian people. In 1901 Congress declared that all Indians in the Indian Territory were U.S. rather than tribal citizens, putting them on the same legal footing as whites in the Oklahoma Territory. In 1907 the Oklahoma and Indian territories were combined into a new state, Oklahoma. Many Indian groups, such as the Keetoowah Cherokees, continued to resist the legality of the dissolution of their tribal status, and Indian people throughout Oklahoma worked to restore their tribal status, tribal governments, and ownership of communal land.

Pan-Indian Organizations

One consequence of continued threats to Indian land and sovereignty—and the attendance of thousands of Indians at boarding schools—was that diverse Indian peoples gained a common language of communication through English and a gathering place where Indian people from all

....

A 1914 banquet of the Society of the American Indians, composed of educated Indians.

1903

January 5 In the U.S. Supreme Court, *Lone Wolf v. Hitchcock* asserts that the U.S. Congress has plenary power over Indian affairs.

Kiowa chief Lone Wolf sues U.S. Secretary of the Interior Ethan Hitchcock to prevent the breakup of Kiowa lands under the allotment policy.

1904

September 21 Chief Joseph dies while living with relatives and followers on the Colville Indian Reservation in Washington State.

1906

May 8 U.S. Congress passes the Burke Act, which amends the Dawes Allotment Act to allow Indians to sell their allotments at any time.

1907

Congress authorizes Indian Affairs commissioner Francis Leupp to sell the allotments of land belonging to Indians deemed "non-competent."

November 16 Congress unites the Oklahoma and Indian territories to create the new state of Oklahoma.

over the country could discuss their experiences and problems. Indian political leaders and graduates from boarding schools began forming new pan-Indian organizations, made up of members of dozens of tribes, in order to address common needs and apply pressure on elected officials. One of the first such organizations was the Society of American Indians (SAI), formed at Ohio State University in 1911 by educated Indian men and women. Carlos Montezuma, a Yavapai Indian, was one of the men who cofounded the SAI. After earning a degree in chemistry from the University of Illinois in the mid-1880s, Montezuma completed his medical training at the Chicago Medical College in 1889. He served as a doctor at the Carlisle Indian School for three years and in private practice, but his greatest accomplishment was in getting the Fort McDowell Indian Reservation established among the Yavapai people. The SAI provided a forum where Indian concerns and problems could be discussed on a national scale, and it published a newspaper, but internal squabbles led to its dissolution in the 1920s. The Native American Church was established in Oklahoma as a nonprofit organization in 1918.

The Native American Church movement had existed on the southern plains since at least the 1890s and was promoted most unflinchingly by Comanche leader Quanah Parker. Parker taught that taking peyote and following the "Peyote Road" would lead Indians to the teachings of Jesus Christ through visions.

Another prominent American Indian of the early twentieth century was a Sauk man, Jim Thorpe. He had attended Carlisle Indian School in Pennsylvania and became a star athlete in football, baseball, and track and field. Thorpe won gold medals in the decathlon and pentathlon in the 1912 Olympic Games held in Stockholm, Sweden. However, because he had played semiprofessional baseball in 1909, he was stripped of his Olympic medals (they were not restored until 1983, thirty years after his death). Thorpe also played professional football and baseball well into the 1920s.

Most Indian organizations formed in the early twentieth century addressed local concerns. The Northwest Federation of

Comanche chief Quanah Parker founded the Native American Church in the early twentieth century.

1908

January 6 The U.S. Supreme Court case *Winters v. United States* formalizes the doctrine of reserved water rights for Indian reservations.

1909

February 17 Geronimo dies, never having been allowed to return to his homeland.

1910

Winnebago man Henry Roe Cloud earns a B.A. degree from Yale University.

1911

February 23 Comanche leader Quanah Parker dies.

October 12 Yavapai man Carlos Montezuma cofounds the Society of American Indians pan-Indian organization in Columbus, Ohio.

American Indians was founded in 1914 by members of tribes and bands around Puget Sound to defend tribal fishing rights. In 1922 the All-Pueblo Council formed in New Mexico to protect Pueblo control over land. That same year, the Navajo Tribal Council was set up to bring leaders from the widely dispersed Navajo communities together to make collective decisions. New England Indians came together in 1928 as the Wampanoag Nation to publicize the continued existence of Indians in the area and to seek protection of Indian rights.

Indians in World War I

When the United States entered World War I in April 1917, special draft boards to recruit American Indian soldiers were set up throughout the country. Nearly 12,000 Indian men registered for service, and 6,500 were called

up to serve. Indian women joined the Red Cross, replaced Indian Office staffers who joined the war effort, and served as nurses in Europe. Although few Indian soldiers became officers, they served in every major engagement where the U.S. Army participated. Several Indian soldiers received awards for their service during battle, and nearly 5 percent of Indian soldiers who saw combat died. American Indian service in the war gave Indians the opportunity to show that they were just as patriotic as other Americans, and Congress granted automatic U.S. citizenship to all Indian veterans in 1919. Subsequently, this was granted in 1924 to all other Indians who had not yet received it, but Indian people still confronted

....
Sauk Indian Jim Thorpe was a star athlete in baseball, football, and track and field.

entrenched stereotypes about their belief systems and lifestyles.

Living Conditions

In the first few decades of the twentieth century, the survival of Indian people seemed in doubt. Their overall population, according to the U.S. census, reached its lowest point in 1900 with around 250,000 Indians living in the country. Government officials assumed that the allotment policy and boarding schools forced on most tribes would quickly force them to assimilate into American society as small farmers and domestic workers, but the reality was that most Indian people experienced a life of crippling poverty. In the *Winters v. United States* decision of 1908, the U.S. Supreme Court supported the notion that western Indians should become farmers while ironically strengthening Indian claims to sovereignty. A white farmer named Henry Winters sought water rights upstream of the Fort Belknap Reservation in Montana, which was inhabited by the Gros Ventres and Assiniboines. The court said that Congress would not have set up reservations for the purpose of promoting farming and then denied

---

1912

July 7 Sauk man Jim Thorpe wins two gold medals at the Olympic Games. He is heralded as the greatest male athlete of the first half of the twentieth century by the Associated Press.

1913-1932

Duncan Campbell Scott becomes Deputy Superintendent General of the Department of Indian Affairs in Canada.

1914

Ojibwa professional baseball player Charles Albert Bender ends his career with the Philadelphia Athletics.

1916

Dakota man Charles Eastman publishes his autobiography, *From the Deep Woods to Civilization.*

1917

April 6 The United States enters World War I and 12,000 Indians enroll in the armed forces.

Indians use of the water necessary to farm; Indians were thus entitled to first and primary use of water flowing through their reservations. This decision is still in effect today, with far-reaching consequences for the arid West.

In 1928 the Meriam Commission (headed by Lewis Meriam, a staff researcher for the Brookings Institute) issued a report that showed that Indians had not adjusted well to allotment and were experiencing extreme poverty. The commission members visited more than ninety reservations and Indian agencies in a seven-month period. They found that Indian people experienced the highest infant mortality rates; their per capita income was less than $200 a year (the national average was $1,350 a year); their diets lacked fruit and vegetables; common diseases like measles ran rampant; medical facilities—if they existed on a reservation at all—were inadequate; and schools were poorly staffed, unsanitary, and overcrowded. The Meriam Commission Report singled out allotment as the major cause of these conditions and also blamed

....

Carlisle Indian School graduates, who learned how to build ships to support the United States in World War I.

1918

The Native American Church is founded in Oklahoma as a nonprofit organization.

1918–1919 The influenza epidemic that sweeps through the world also kills tens of thousands of Indian people on reservations throughout the United States.

1919

November 6 The U.S. government grants citizenship to all American Indian veterans of World War I.

1922

The League of Indians of Canada is founded by 1,500 Plains Indians at the Samson Reserve in Alberta to demand larger grants from the Canadian government.

Oil is discovered on Navajo land in Arizona. The Standard Oil Company wants access to the oil through the Bureau of Indian Affairs.

The All-Pueblo Council is formed by Pueblo political leaders in New Mexico to combat the Bursum Bill in U.S. Congress.

Secretary of the Interior and former senator Albert Fall supports legislation to open up more Indian lands in New Mexico to white settlement.

The Bureau of Indian Affairs convinces Navajos to organize the first Navajo Tribal Council to provide low-cost leases to energy companies.

November 24 The U.S. government mediates the negotiation of the Colorado River Basin Compact by western states to share the waters of the Colorado River.

the Bureau of Indian Affairs (BIA) and Congress for failing to adequately administer and fund programs for Indians. The only living for many Indians came from selling or leasing their allotted lands, which provided temporary income but did not promote self-sufficiency. The major impact of the Meriam Report was that it pointed out the obvious need to dramatically reform Indian affairs in the United States.

The Indian New Deal

When the Great Depression struck the United States and the world in the late 1920s, Indian people welcomed much of the rest of America to their living status. When Franklin D. Roosevelt and his New Deal were elected in 1932, reform of the Indian Office became a top priority. John Collier became commissioner of Indian Affairs in April 1933 and oversaw a remarkable shift in U.S. Indian policy. He had long worked with American Indians in the Southwest and urged reforms of the Indian Office. In 1933 Collier, along with new Secretary of the Interior Harold

An Assiniboine medicine man from the Fort Belknap reservation in Montana in the early 1900s.

Ickes, enacted many of the reforms called for in the Meriam Report, especially the overturning of the Dawes Act legislation. He emphasized a new outlook with regard to Indians and announced that the federal government was willing to try new approaches to solve the entrenched problems that Indians faced. Taking advantage of the slate of New Deal legislation being passed by the Democratic Congress in Roosevelt's first hundred days in office, Collier crafted the Indian Emergency Conservation work program, an Indian version of the New Deal's Civilian Conservation Corps. Indians dug wells, planted trees, and built roads, dams, fences, erosion control projects, and community centers on reservations. Surplus military gear—such as blankets, cots, and clothing—were distributed to Indians, along with money for reservations and communities to buy cattle. Debts owed by Indians to the federal government were canceled, and more schools and hospitals were built. Collier also ordered his agents to stop requiring Indian attendance at Christian religious services; he was a strong supporter of traditional Indian culture and arts, and sought ways to incubate traditional expressions and beliefs.

1923

John Collier and others form the American Indian Defense Association.

1924

The Indian Oil Leasing Act is passed by the U.S. Congress. This act grants energy companies longer leases to extract oil from Indian lands.

The U.S. government establishes the Indian Health Division within the Bureau of Indian Affairs in an attempt to address the rampant health problems among reservation Indians.

June 2 Congress grants U.S. citizenship to all Indians not previously made citizens by earlier legislation.

Virginia passes the Racial Integrity Law that redefines many of the state's Indians as "Negro."

Several pieces of New Deal legislation that dealt specifically with Indian matters passed through Congress at Collier's urging. The most far-reaching new law was the Indian Reorganization Act (IRA) of 1934. Collier's original proposal to transfer much of the governing power from the federal government to Indian tribal governments became watered down during debates in Congress and within Indian tribes (the original forty-eight pages of proposed legislation became, in the end, just five pages), but the final legislation still heralded a new direction in U.S.-Indian affairs. The final version of the IRA dealt primarily with Indian self-government and increased federal support. Most important, the U.S. government officially abandoned allotment. Next, the IRA granted Indian communities the right to establish new constitutional governments to manage as much of their own affairs as possible within the confines of existing federal law. Collier helped to craft the constitutions to make sure they were modeled after the U.S. Constitution with an

John Collier tried to convince all Indian groups to adopt the Indian Reorganization Act of 1934.

1925

Indian powwows are banned by the Canadian government.

1927

The Canadian Indian Act is amended to make it illegal for First Nations to raise money or retain a lawyer to advance land claims, thereby blocking effective political court action.

1928

February 21 The Meriam Commission Report on living conditions among American Indians labels the allotment policy a failure.

1930

The U.S. Senate finds that Navajo children have been systematically kidnapped and placed in boarding schools against the wishes of their parents.

1932

September 20 The Paiute prophet Wovoka dies.

elected legislature, or council, and an elected chairman, or chief. The IRA made a permanent loan fund available to Indian tribes to jump-start economic development and funding for education. Indians were not subject to the same civil service exam requirements to serve in the BIA. Finally, the IRA would be brought into effect only if a tribe consented to its approval.

Other Indian New Deal legislation included the Johnson-O'Malley Act of 1934, which funded state schools in providing education to Indian students. Certain districts and states did not always use the money to recruit or serve Indian students directly but, by 1938, 34,000 Indian children were attending state schools, 14,000 went to day schools on reservations, 10,000 were enrolled in boarding schools, and 7,000 attended missionary schools. Congress passed the Indian Arts and Crafts Act in 1935, which established the Indian Arts and Crafts Board. The Arts and Crafts Board established standards of authenticity to promote the production and marketing of Indian art.

Secretary of the Interior Harold Ickes meets with Indian leaders in 1935.

1932–1936

More than 250,000 Navajo sheep and goats are killed on the orders of the U.S. government in the stock reduction policy.

1933

June 15 Lakota man Plenty Horses dies.

President Franklin D. Roosevelt appoints John Collier as the new commissioner of Indian Affairs.

June 18 Congress passes the Indian Emergency Conservation Work program, an Indian version of the New Deal's Civilian Conservation Corps.

1934

April 16 Congress passes the Indian Reorganization Act, which seeks to revolutionize the way Indian groups interact with the U.S. government. The act ends allotment as the official policy of the U.S. government.

Congress passes the Johnson-O'Malley Act to provide more money to local school districts that accept and educate Indian students.

Collier and the act's supporters sought to preserve Indian cultural expressions and to remove exploitative middlemen from the marketing process in order to promote financial gain for the sole use of Indian people. Collier also increased the number of Indians working for the BIA from a few hundred to 4,500 by the late 1930s.

Many Indian tribes and people opposed certain aspects of this New Deal legislation, especially the IRA. In the 1930s, 189 tribes voted to accept the IRA while seventy-seven rejected it. Those who opposed the act condemned it as an "Indian Raw Deal," arguing that it placed Indian governance under even more direct control of the Secretary of the Interior because constitutions had to be approved by the Secretary and the BIA. The Navajos, Californian tribes, Crows, Senecas, other Iroquois groups, and the Lakota Sioux did not initially approve the IRA. The issues differed for each tribe, but generally, splits developed in Indian communities between "progressive" assimilationist Indians and "conservative" traditional Indians over the question of how to govern their communities, with the traditional side being opposed to the IRA and the new form

The New Deal Civilian Conservation Corps put Indians, such as these Tlingit men, to work restoring totem poles in the Tongass National Forest, Alaska.

1935

After votes taken around the country, 189 tribes accept the Indian Reorganization Act and seventy-seven—including the Navajos, Klamaths, Crows, and Senecas—reject it.

Congress passes the Oklahoma Welfare Act to organize tribal governments among the Indian groups in that state.

August 15 Cherokee humorist Will Rogers dies.

August 27 Congress establishes the Indian Arts and Crafts Board to create standards of authenticity and to remove exploitative middlemen from marketing Indian arts and crafts.

1936

May 1 Congress extends the Indian Reorganization Act to Alaska.

of tribal government. In addition, more than 40 percent of Indians in the United States were automatically excluded from the IRA's benefits because they were not members of a federally recognized tribe. Alaska and Oklahoma received their own versions of the IRA through a special piece of legislation.

Collier did not adequately appreciate the complexities of Native American life in the United States, but the IRA did return more than 4 million acres of land to Native control. Tribes who accepted the IRA formed corporations and borrowed money from the federal government, with only a 1 percent default rate by 1945. The IRA allowed dances and other ceremonies that had previously been outlawed, alleviated poverty in some cases, provided educational opportunities, and built housing on many reservations.

The Navajos narrowly turned down the IRA with a vote of 7,608 for and 7,992 against the act. Distrust of the U.S.

....

Indian arts and crafts received protections and support from the Indian Arts and Crafts Act of 1935.

government among the Navajos dated back to the 1860s, when the U.S. Army had forced more than 8,000 Navajos to march 350 miles on the "Long Walk" that killed hundreds of Navajo men, women, and children. More recently, Collier himself had forced the destruction of tens of thousands of Navajo goats and sheep to reduce grazing pressures on the arid land of the Navajo reservation. Soil erosion had become a serious problem and silt had built up behind a government-financed dam on the reservation, threatening the reservoir. Navajo families depended on their goat and sheep herds to survive; the animals provided meat for their personal consumption and wool for making rugs and blankets to be sold to outsiders. The U.S. government had argued that the drastic policy was necessary to prevent soil erosion, but sheep provided the backbone of the Navajo economy and had done so ever since the Spanish introduced sheep in the seventeenth century. The Navajos never understood the rationale for the slaughter of their animals and refused to cooperate with later U.S. government demands to enact a new constitutional government. The Navajos also already had a tribal government,

1937

The Navajo Tribal Council is formed. Despite rejecting the Indian Reorganization Act, the Navajos create a new tribal government at the insistence of the Bureau of Indian Affairs.

1938

May 11 Congress passes the Indian Lands Mining Act, which authorizes the Secretary of the Interior to issue leases on Indian land to energy companies.

1939

May 13 The Tonawanda Indian community house is constructed on the Seneca Indian Tonawanda Reservation in New York.

1939–1945

During World War II, nearly 25,000 American Indian men serve in the armed forces and at least 40,000 Indians leave home to take war-related jobs.

1941

December 7 The Japanese attack on Pearl Harbor brings the United States into World War II.

December 7 Choctaw sailor Henry Nolatubby dies on the USS *Arizona* during the Japanese bombardment of Pearl Harbor.

which they strengthened on their own in 1938 by electing a tribal chairman and moving into a new U.S. government-financed headquarters building on the reservation at Window Rock.

Indians in World War II

One-third of all eligible Indian males and around 800 Indian women joined the armed forces to serve in World War II. Nearly 40,000 other Indian men and 8,000 Indian women also participated in the wartime industries and moved to cities to work in factories. The government required all American Indian men to register for military conscription, even though they could not vote in many states. Many Indians refused to register. The Seminoles declared they were still at war with the United States; the Iroquois objected because they did not consider themselves to be U.S. citizens; and the Papagos refused because they followed a religion of nonviolence.

The U.S. Marines established a Navajo code talker unit of around 400 Navajos to serve in

A meeting of Navajos near Window Rock in 1938. The Navajos rejected Collier's Indian Reorganization Act.

1941–1945

Crow Indian man Joseph Medicine Crow serves in the U.S. Army in Europe during World War II. While fighting against the Germans, he accomplishes the four deeds necessary to be a traditional chief of the Crow tribe.

The government requires all American Indian men in the United States to register for military conscription, even though they are not allowed to vote in many states.

1942

March Japanese internment camps in Arizona are established on lands taken from the Pima and Mohave Indian reservations.

June 12 The Iroquois Nation declares war on Germany separately from the United States in order to emphasize their sovereignty.

September U.S. Marines establish a Navajo code talker unit of around 400 Navajos, which serves in the Pacific fighting against the Japanese.

The U.S. government seizes an estimated 900,000 acres from Indians in Alaska and from Indian reservations in the West to establish military bases, gunnery ranges, and nuclear test sites.

the Pacific against the Japanese. The bilingual Navajo men devised a code in their native language for use in radio communications, which was never broken by the Japanese. Other Indian military personnel, such as the Comanches and Choctaws, also used their native languages in radio communications to confuse the Germans and Japanese. A Crow Indian, Joseph Medicine Crow, served in the U.S. Army in Europe. While fighting against the Germans, he accomplished the four deeds necessary to be a traditional chief of the Crow tribe: counting coup (touching an enemy soldier), stealing horses from the enemy, leading men in a successful battle, and capturing or killing enemy forces. Since his return to Montana after the war, he has served as the Crow tribe's historian and anthropologist and authored several essays and books. He earned an M.A. degree in anthropology from the University of Southern California in 1939. Other Native American heroes of the war include Admiral Joseph Clark, a Cherokee, the first Indian to attend the Annapolis Naval

In World War II, Navajo code talkers used their language and a new code to send radio signals.

1943

September 22 Although wounded, Creek Indian Ernest Childers kills five enemy soldiers and captures one other while eliminating a machine-gun nest in fighting near Oliveto, Italy.

1944

April 8 Ernest Childers is given the Congressional Medal of Honor.

November Salish Indian D'Arcy McNickle helps to establish the National Congress of American Indians.

November The National Congress of American Indians is formed in Denver, Colorado.

Academy, and Air Force general Clarence Tinker, an Osage Indian, who was shot down during the Battle of Midway. Although wounded, Creek Indian Ernest Childers killed five enemy soldiers and captured another while eliminating a machine-gun nest in fighting near Oliveto, Italy; Childers earned the Congressional Medal of Honor for his efforts.

Ira Hayes, a Pima Indian, returned to the United States a war hero after service in the U.S. Marines, including participation in the unit that raised the American flag on Mount Suribachi on Iwo Jima in 1945, made famous in photographs and newsreel footage. Sent around the country by the U.S. government to promote the selling of war bonds, Hayes found readjusting to civilian life difficult. Back on the Pima reservation in Arizona, he encountered both racism and discrimination, such as not being allowed to vote according to state law. After a few years, he succumbed to alcoholism and died. When most Indians returned from the war, they too encountered poverty and unemployment, as

A World War II bond poster. Nearly a third of all eligible Indian men joined the forces during the war.

A 1943 picture of Lieutenant Ernest Childers, a member of the Creek tribe from Oklahoma.

well as rampant racism despite their recent service to the United States. At the same time, the federal government was trying once again to change its relationship with Indian tribes in what became known as the Termination Policy.

Termination and Relocation

In the post–World War II era—an age of rampant anti-Communism characterized by the House

---

1945

April 12 President Roosevelt dies in office and is replaced by Harry Truman. John Collier, head of the Bureau of Indian Affairs, resigns and the Indian New Deal ends.

Germany surrenders to the Allies in May and Japan surrenders in August.

May 10 Pima Indian Ira Hayes returns to the United States a war hero after service in the U.S. Marines, which included participation in the unit that raised the flag at the Battle of Iwo Jima.

1946

August 10 The United Keetoowah Band of the Cherokees is recognized by the Bureau of Indian Affairs.

August 13 After lobbying from the National Congress of American Indians, Congress establishes the Indian Claims Commission to hear and settle claims from Indian groups about land taken by the United States without proper authority or compensation.

Un-American Activities Committee and the accusations of Senator Joseph McCarthy—Indian groups encountered new threats to their sovereignty. After the war, the ideological emphasis was on conforming to American ideals of capitalism, individualism, and Christianity. Reservations were equated in some officials' minds with communal life, which in turn was equated with Communism. In 1949 the Hoover Commission, led by former President Herbert Hoover, recommended that the federal government should "terminate" its relationship with Indian tribes and force Indians to integrate into American society as American citizens. John Collier had resigned as head of the BIA in 1945 under intense pressure toward his policies and personal attacks on his motives. Almost immediately, Collier's policies, on which he had worked so hard during the New Deal, were overturned. The federal government now sought to terminate its relationship with Indian tribes once and for all by forcing Indians into the mainstream, sending them to cities, and breaking up communally held land on reservations.

....

The anti-Communist hysteria after World War II impacted Indians, since it prompted new policies.

1947

Postwar reclamation projects by the U.S. government dam up rivers, inundating Indian reservation lands along the Columbia, Snake, and Missouri rivers.

The U.S. government completes a survey of mineral resources available on Indian-owned land. Many western Indian reservations contain vast amounts of coal, oil, natural gas, or uranium.

1948

Seneca woman Alice Lee Jemison speaks to Congress in opposition to the new policy of termination.

1949

The Hoover Commission recommends that the federal government should "terminate" its relationship with Indian tribes and force Indians to integrate into American society as American citizens.

1950

Dillon Myer, a supporter of the termination policy, becomes Commissioner of Indian Affairs. He announces a new policy of Indian relocation to cities.

In 1950 Dillon S. Myer, a supporter of the termination policy who had overseen the forced relocation of Japanese-Americans to internment camps during World War II, became Commissioner of Indian Affairs. He announced a new policy of relocation whereby Indian people received one-way bus tickets and minimal assistance to move off reservations and into cities. Thousands of Indian people around the country took advantage of the offer in search of jobs, but they found it difficult to adjust to city life and many returned to the reservations. The goal of relocation was to move Indians into the mainstream by putting them in cities; many Indians had already moved to cities during World War II. Relocated Indians encountered language barriers, lack of job skills, greater violence, and racism. Many returned to reservations rather than deal with life in the cities, but by 1960 about one-third of all Indians lived in cities—a proportion that has grown since then.

Indian Claims Commission

In 1946, after lobbying from the National Congress of American Indians (NCAI), Congress established the Indian Claims Commission (ICC) to hear and settle claims from Indian groups about land taken by the U.S. government over the years without either proper authority or compensation. The U.S. government now admitted that more than 370 of the treaties it had negotiated with Indian tribes were flawed, and promised that the ICC would seek to pay Indians—once and for all—for lands taken. In addition, the BIA was eventually to be disbanded and the special relationship between the federal government and Indian groups would end. Despite the good intentions, the process became fraught with difficulties: a tribe had to prove its original ownership of land with the aid of outside historians and anthropologists rather than their own oral traditions. If a tribe won a claim, it could be compensated only with money, not a return of land, and the value of the land was determined from the value at the time that the government had acquired the territory, not mid-twentieth-century values. Costs for the ICC proceedings were then subtracted to derive a final payout amount. Indian tribes who claimed areas that were now major metropolitan areas, such as Los Angeles,

In 1949 Herbert Hoover led a government commission that recommended the U.S. government terminate its relationships with Indian groups.

1951

The Canadian government repeals the Indian Act provisions that outlaw potlatch and powwows, as well as land claims activity.

1952

The largest open-pit uranium mine in the world begins operation at the Laguna pueblo in New Mexico.

1953

August 1 Termination becomes official U.S. Indian policy through House Concurrent Resolution 108. The U.S. government moves to end the special status of Indian tribes.

August 15 Public Law 280 unilaterally extends state jurisdiction over Indian affairs in California, Minnesota, Nebraska, Oregon, and Wisconsin.

The Chicago American Indian Center is established as the first urban Indian center in the United States.

rejected settlement because the amount of money they were to receive—just twelve cents a hectare in some cases—did not come close to matching the mid-twentieth-century value of the land. Other questions arose over who should receive portions of the payout. The ICC disbanded in 1978 after deciding on 484 cases, with 285 of those being decided in favor of the Indian plaintiffs.

Once a tribe had accepted ICC money, the U.S. government sought to terminate its relationship with that Indian tribe once and for all. In 1953 termination became the official U.S. Indian policy through House Concurrent Resolution 108. The government moved to end the special status of Indian tribes and people by removing federal support and regulation of Indian tribes. Two weeks later, President Eisenhower signed Public Law 280, which abolished tribal courts and police systems on all reservations in California, Minnesota, Wisconsin, Nebraska, and Oregon. The law gave those states jurisdiction over Indian affairs

The National Congress of American Indians lobbied against the termination policies of the U.S. government.

1954

August 13 The Klamaths of Oregon are terminated by the U.S. government, removing all federal support and making them subject to state jurisdiction.

November 21 Coeur d'Alene Indian Joe Garry is elected president of the National Congress of American Indians and leads the organization in opposition to the termination policy.

Anthropologists and historians form a new academic organization called the American Indian Ethnohistoric Conference.

1955

January 1 Seneca anthropologist Arthur C. Parker dies.

1957

The Tuscaroras refuse permission to the New York Power Authority to take soil tests on their reservation lands.

within their borders and removed federal jurisdiction. New York State had already acquired state jurisdiction over Indians in special legislation passed in 1948. These states pursued policies to disband reservations and open up land and natural resources to the highest bidder. This new legislation called for gradual termination, especially of tribes that were doing "well" economically. BIA Commissioner Dillon Myer, Senator Arthur Watkins (a Republican from Utah), and Congressman E. Y. Berry of South Dakota supported this legislation because they agreed with interests in their states that wanted easier access to Indian lands and resources. Between 1954 and 1962, the government imposed termination on sixty-one tribes, the most significant being the Menominees in Wisconsin and the Klamaths in Oregon.

Both the Klamath and Menominee tribes suffered rampant unemployment and escalation of suicide and alcoholism rates as their sources of income from timber cultivation dried up and

President Harry Truman signed the Indian Claims Commission into law in 1946.

1958

April Tuscarora women in New York lay down in the road to prevent surveyors from trying to seize more than a thousand acres through eminent domain.

January 18 Lumbee Indians in North Carolina drive off a planned Ku Klux Klan rally by arming themselves and daring the Klan members to appear.

1959

January 12 The U.S. Supreme Court case *Williams v. Lee* proclaims that state jurisdiction does not extend into Indian country.

A Choctaw man, Philip Martin, becomes chief of the Mississippi Band of Choctaw Indians.

1960

First Nations people in Canada gain the right to vote in federal elections.

their communal lands disappeared. The Klamaths ran a successful timber mill that provided a living, and they owned nearly one million acres of prime northwestern timber land. The Klamaths had filed an ICC claim and won. However, Senator Watkins told the people that they must accept termination before their money would be disbursed. Klamath termination occurred in June 1954 and was a disaster. The reservation was disbanded and made into a state county. The federal government removed its support for education and health care. Most of the Klamath people became enmeshed in poverty and drifted away to seek work in cities like Portland and San Francisco. Rates of alcoholism and domestic violence soared, and traditions were forgotten. Eventually, in 1986, the Klamaths regained tribal status, but the severe damage of the termination experience has never been overcome.

Menominee termination came into effect in 1961. The timber mill became a corporation in which whites controlled much of the stock. The mill had relied on favorable contract positions from its status as a tribal enterprise and those guarantees of business disappeared. The mill

President Eisenhower signed Public Law 280, which ended Indian tribal sovereignty in many western states.

Ada Deer successfully fought to reestablish Menominee tribal status after it had been terminated in 1961.

corporation fired workers and sold forest lands to cover debts and taxes to the state. Moreover, the Menominee people now had to pay state taxes, to which they were not subject previously. The area quickly became the poorest county in the state, and the health center had to close due to lack of funding and poor conditions. As Menominee termination came into full effect and the reservation became a county in the state

---

1961

Menominee termination comes into full effect and the Menominee reservation becomes a county in the state of Wisconsin.

June 13–20 University of Chicago anthropologist Sol Tax brings Indian leaders together from seventy-nine tribes throughout the United States to discuss issues that affect all Indians. The American Indian Chicago Conference issues a Declaration of Indian Purpose, calling termination a great threat to Indian survival.

Menominee social worker Ada Deer campaigns tirelessly for restoration of tribal government and trust status with the U.S. government.

August 10 The National Indian Youth Council is founded in New Mexico.

1961–1972

"Fish-ins" occur in the state of Washington as Puyallup-Nisqually fishermen insist on fishing in a traditional manner with large nets.

A Menominee man sharpening a saw in 1941. Menominee success in the timber industry in Wisconsin made them a target for termination.

of Wisconsin, Menominee people led by a female social worker named Ada Deer campaigned tirelessly for restoration of their tribal government and trust status with the U.S. government. Deer's efforts paid off in 1973, when the Menominee tribe was restored to tribal status. Deer remained active in politics and served as head of the BIA from 1993 to 1997.

Energy Issues

Despite being placed on "worthless" reservations, many Native people controlled land that contained huge quantities of minerals and underground water. One-third of western coal, one-fifth of the natural gas, and one-half of the uranium deposits in the United States are on Indian land, especially Indian reservations in the West. The initial modern assault on Indian-held natural resources followed the discovery of oil in Oklahoma in 1882. Beginning in the 1890s, the U.S. government allowed Indian lands to be leased for mining. The existence of reservations provided a convenient way to exploit Indian-held natural resources in the twentieth century. Contracts only had to be negotiated with tribal councils (which were largely a New Deal

1962

The Institute of American Indian Art is founded in Santa Fe, New Mexico, by Indian artists and students.

The U.S. government under President Kennedy abandons the termination policy.

1964

A Standing Rock Sioux man, Vine Deloria Jr., becomes executive director of the National Congress of American Indians, a position he holds until 1967.

August 24 In the California Supreme Court case *People v. Woody*, the court rules that prosecuting an Indian member of the Native American Church for possession of peyote is unconstitutional.

1965

September Canadian Iroquois chief Alexander General dies.

Alaskan Natives meet and create the Alaska Federated Natives organization to pursue land claims on behalf of Alaskan Native people.

A Klamath Indian man guiding logs in Oregon before the termination policy destroyed Klamath sovereignty and economic viability in 1954.

1966

Kiowa author N. Scott Momaday publishes the novel *House Made of Dawn*, which wins the Pulitzer Prize for Literature in 1968.

The American Indian Ethnohistoric Conference changes its name to the American Society for Ethnohistory.

Black Mesa on the Navajo reservation is mined by the Peabody Coal Company.

1968

The U.S. Congress passes the Indian Civil Rights Act sponsored by North Carolina Senator Sam Ervin Jr.

July 28 The American Indian Movement is founded in Minneapolis by urban Indians.

development) or with the BIA, which acted on behalf of Indian tribes, although not always in their best interests. This system enabled energy companies to get access to Indian land and natural resources relatively easily; however, the impact of loss of resources and pollution on Indian people proved devastating in the long term.

In 1947 the U.S. government completed a survey of mineral resources available on Indian-owned land. Many western Indian reservations contained vast amounts of coal, oil, natural gas, or uranium, and energy companies worked through the BIA to gain access to those resources. Exploitation of natural resources promised jobs and some income on Indian reservations, but the leases negotiated on behalf of Indians by the BIA often failed to acquire fair compensation for Indians or provide for the cleanup of pollution caused by mining and drilling. The conflicts that have arisen over exploitation of natural resources on Indian land are sometimes called the "New Indian Wars."

In 1957 New York Iroquois tribes responded with increased militancy to threats to their reservation lands. The Tuscaroras refused permission to the New York Power Authority to take soil tests on their reservation lands, and Tuscarora women lay down in the road to prevent surveyors from trying to seize over a thousand acres. The land was seized anyway, but the Tuscaroras did win a lawsuit the next year that required the New York Power Authority to pay them $13 million. Senecas resisted the planned construction of the Kinzua Dam that flooded 10,000 acres of their land by the time of its completion in 1961, but the U.S. government forced them to move to new settlements.

The Navajos have perhaps suffered from the war over energy resources to a higher degree than any other tribe. Their reservation contains huge amounts of uranium, which became a highly sought-after commodity with the development of nuclear weapons and electrical power after World War II. The nuclear arms race and the building of nuclear power plants required ever greater amounts of uranium and brought energy companies to the Navajo

The discovery of oil underneath Indian land quickened the demand for access to Indian lands.

1969

January 1 The Canadian government's White Paper on Indian policy calls for a new direction in Canadian-Indian relations to address the needs of Indian people.

Laguna Pueblo author Leslie Marmon Silko graduates from the University of New Mexico.

1969–1971

November 1969–June 1971 Alcatraz Island in San Francisco Bay is occupied by Indian people calling themselves "Indians of All Tribes" in order to bring awareness to Indian issues.

Richard Oakes, a Mohawk man, plays an integral role in organizing the Alcatraz occupation. He creates one of the first Native American Studies programs in the country at San Francisco State University.

Scientists test for uranium deposits on Indian land in 1951.

reservation. In 1952 the Navajo council accepted (under BIA pressure) a contract with the Kerr-McGee Company to mine uranium. Publicity about the deal touted the employment of Indians, thereby helping to bring about better economic conditions on the reservation. However, the company employed only about 150 Navajos, at a lower rate of pay than non-Navajo workers. The company failed to adequately implement pollution controls, such as ventilation fans in shafts, and a 1959 government inspection showed that radiation levels in the mines were ninety to a hundred times the maximum permissible for worker safety. In 1970 Kerr-McGee left the Navajo reservation temporarily, leaving Navajo workers unemployed and without health insurance. The company left behind seventy acres of radioactive uranium tailings, and the BIA had omitted to negotiate a cleanup clause in the original contract. By 1980 thirty-eight of the Navajo miners had died of lung cancer and ninety-five more had the disease. The tailings leaked into the San Juan

1970

July 8 President Nixon's message to Congress calls for a new era of Indian self-determination and formally brings an end to the termination policy.

November 26 Russell Means, a Lakota man, becomes known to the American public through his leadership in the *Mayflower* occupation.

November 26 Indian activists and members of the American Indian Movement occupy the *Mayflower* replica in Plymouth, Massachusetts, on Thanksgiving, and Thanksgiving itself is declared to be a day of national mourning.

December 15 Blue Lake is returned by the U.S. government to the Taos pueblo in northern New Mexico. The Taos pueblo regains nearly 48,000 acres that they consider sacred.

A coal mine run by the Peabody Coal Company on the Navajo reservation at Black Mesa, Arizona.

River, a major source of drinking water for people and livestock on the reservation, and birth defects linked to radiation exposure increased dramatically.

Hopi Land Settlement Act

In 1966 the Peabody Coal Company signed a contract to mine at Black Mesa on the Navajo and Hopi reservations, a site considered sacred by both groups. The Navajos and Hopis earned well below market value for the coal that Peabody extracted, and court battles over who had jurisdiction over the area erupted almost immediately. In 1974 Congress passed the Hopi Land Settlement Act, which meant that 12,000 Navajos who lived over the coal deposits in the Hopi-Navajo Joint Use Area on Black Mesa were forced to move. The Peabody Coal Company sought and received access to the land that the Navajos were forced to abandon.

On July 16, 1979, the largest nuclear accident in the history of the United States released more than 1,100 tons of radioactive waste into the Rio Puerco, a major source of drinking water for people and livestock on the Navajo reservation. Livestock in the area

1971

July 4 The American Indian Movement occupies Mount Rushmore in South Dakota to protest against American "desecration" of the Black Hills.

The Native American Rights Fund is established to provide legal assistance to Native tribes on a range of issues.

Blackfeet/Gros Ventre author James Welch publishes his first book of poetry, *Riding the Earthboy 40*.

December 18 The U.S. Congress approves the Alaska Native Claims Settlement Act.

1972

March The American Indian Movement holds protests in Gordon, Nebraska, over the murder of a Lakota man named Raymond Yellow Thunder.

November 3 The American Indian Movement sponsors the Trail of Broken Treaties national protest that culminated in the occupation of the Bureau of Indian Affairs building in Washington, D.C.

quickly developed sores and died, and people were ordered not to drink the water, which was 6,000 times above the safe drinking water level for radioactivity. The United Nuclear Company owned the sludge pond whose dam had failed, but the U.S. Environmental Protection Agency picked up the tab for the partial cleanup of the extremely radioactive river system.

Meanwhile, other Indian groups also suffered through horrendous pollution and mistreatment by energy companies. In 1952 the Anaconda Copper Company began mining uranium in an open-pit mine at the Laguna pueblo in New Mexico. By 1980 the Jackpile Mine, as it was called, was the largest open-pit uranium mine in the world, encompassing some 2,800 acres. The company discharged more than 500 million gallons of radioactive water and left a 260-acre radioactive tailings pile. All water at the Laguna pueblo was contaminated, and Anaconda used pulverized low-grade uranium ore in the gravel used to pave roads and construct buildings, making them radioactive.

Mining on Indian reservations has resulted in pollution and health problems, while also bringing in income.

1973

February 28 The American Indian Movement occupies Wounded Knee, site of the 1890 massacre of Big Foot's people. The standoff lasts seventy-one days and two American Indian supporters are killed.

December 22 The Menominee tribe is restored to federally recognized tribal status.

1974

February 7 Russell Means runs against Richard Wilson for the chairmanship of the Pine Ridge reservation. He loses by fewer than a hundred votes.

November Peter MacDonald is elected chairman of the Navajo tribe.

February 12 In the U.S. Supreme Court case *United States v. Washington* (also called the "Boldt decision"), the court rules in favor of Indian fishing rights in the Northwest.

December 22 The U.S. Congress passes the Hopi Land Settlement Act, forcing more than 12,000 Navajos who lived over the coal deposits in the Hopi-Navajo Joint Use Area to move.

Women of All Red Nations is founded to focus on and empower the traditional role of Native women as leaders within their communities.

In 1971 Congress approved the Alaska Native Claims Settlement Act. Native peoples were compensated for formally ceding millions of acres to the United States, and 220 Native village corporations and twelve regional corporations were established to aid Alaskan Native peoples in negotiating with energy and other companies that sought access to their lands and resources.

Council of Energy Resource Tribes

In response to these types of developments, a coalition of western Indian tribes formed the Council of Energy Resource Tribes (CERT) to negotiate collectively from a position of strength with energy companies that sought access to their natural resources. A Navajo man, Peter MacDonald, became the first chairman of CERT. A code talker during World War II, MacDonald served as tribal chairman of the Navajo Nation from 1974 to 1989. In 1989 he was relieved of his chairmanship position by the Navajo Tribal Council to

Laguna Pueblo in New Mexico is the site of the largest open-pit uranium mine in the world.

answer corruption charges stemming from a 1986 land deal. MacDonald organized his supporters and they stormed the tribal headquarters on July 20, 1989, leading to the deaths of two of his supporters. In 1993 MacDonald was sentenced to fourteen years in

prison for inciting a riot and for racketeering and corruption charges. In January 2001, he was pardoned by outgoing U.S. president Bill Clinton. CERT was modeled on OPEC to give individual tribes a unified voice, enabling them to negotiate adequate contracts with energy

1974–1977

Pine Ridge tribal chairman Richard Wilson's police force initiates a terror campaign against the American Indian Movement and his political opponents.

1975

January 4 The U.S. Congress passes the Indian Self-Determination and Education Assistance Act, which puts resources and more financial authority in the hands of Indian tribes.

Peter MacDonald becomes the first chairman of the Council of Energy Resource Tribes.

June 26 Two FBI agents are killed when they pursue a suspect allegedly belonging to the American Indian Movement on the Pine Ridge reservation in South Dakota.

A coalition of western Indian tribes forms the Council of Energy Resource Tribes to negotiate collectively with energy companies that are seeking access to their natural resources.

1976

February 24 A Micmac woman, Anna Mae Aquash, is found murdered on the Pine Ridge reservation in South Dakota. Aquash was a tireless advocate for Native rights.

companies. Energy companies responded by pouring millions of dollars into CERT and its board members, using the organization to circumvent the necessity of negotiating with individual tribes. The paradox is that Indian reservations need income and jobs, and they must balance the social needs of their communities with maintaining healthy living conditions free from pollution while preserving their land base to ensure their future existence.

Indian Activism and "Red Power"

The termination policy, growing awareness of resource exploitation and pollution, and poor treatment of Indian people inspired Native American activists to get organized in opposition to the further erosion of tribal sovereignty. A Salish Indian, D'Arcy McNickle, helped to establish the National Congress of American Indians (NCAI) in Denver in 1944. McNickle had worked for John Collier at the BIA in the cause of advancing Indian rights and preservation of Indian culture. A prolific writer, McNickle

....

Former Navajo tribal chairman Peter McDonald tried to negotiate better contracts with energy companies.

published several histories and works of literature. He served as the first director of the Newberry Library Center for the History of the American Indian in Chicago. Made up of Indian leaders from throughout the United States, the NCAI promoted Indian civil rights, the preservation of traditional culture, and the safeguarding of Indian lands. In the 1950s, the NCAI worked to overturn the termination policy. The American Indian Chicago Conference, organized by University of Chicago anthropologist Sol Tax in 1961 with the assistance of the NCAI, brought Indian leaders together from seventy-nine tribes throughout the country to discuss issues that affected all Indians. They issued a "Declaration of Indian Purpose" and presented it to President Kennedy, calling termination the greatest threat to Indian survival since the military conflicts of the nineteenth century.

Also in 1961, the National Indian Youth Council (NIYC) was founded in New Mexico with representatives from Indian groups from all over the country to promote Indian education, health, employment, social services, and economic development. "Fish-ins" occurred in the state of Washington as Puyallup-Nisqually

1977

Leslie Marmon Silko's novel *Ceremony* is published.

June 1 An Anishinabe man, Leonard Peltier, is convicted on dubious evidence of murdering two FBI agents on the Pine Ridge reservation in 1975.

November 29 Santa Clara pueblo member Julia Martinez sues her tribe for denying membership to her children, whose father was not a Santa Clara member.

1978

March 6 The U.S. Supreme Court case *Oliphant v. Suquamish* rules that Indian tribes do not hold criminal jurisdiction over non-Indians accused of crimes on Indian land.

Congress passes the American Indian Child Welfare Act, which dramatically lessens the practice of taking Indian children away from their families and people.

May 15 The U.S. Supreme Court decides in the *Martinez v. Santa Clara* case that Indian tribes control access to their membership.

August 11 The U.S. Congress approves the American Indian Religious Freedom Act, which guarantees freedom of religion for American Indians.

The American Indian Movement and other Indian activists stage the Longest Walk from San Francisco to Washington, D.C., to bring public attention to areas of need in Indian communities.

fishermen insisted on fishing in a traditional manner with large nets. Although treaties with the U.S. government had protected the Puyallup-Nisqually right to fish traditionally, the State of Washington tried to enforce new game laws that made such activities illegal. Modeled in part on the strategy of African American civil rights protestors who conducted sit-ins at segregated bus stations and restaurants, the fish-ins similarly garnered national media attention to the struggles of Indian people to retain their civil rights. By 1966 national celebrities such as Marlon Brando and Dick Gregory joined the fish-ins to bring national attention to the abolishment of treaty rights.

From 1969 to 1972, Native American college students from the San Francisco Bay Area and beyond, calling themselves Indians of All Tribes in order to bring awareness to Indian issues, occupied the abandoned federal prison on Alcatraz Island in San Francisco Bay. Hundreds of Indians traveled back and forth to Alcatraz over the two years of the occupation, which

....

President John F. Kennedy in 1961, the same year of the American Indian Chicago Conference.

empowered them with a sense of accomplishment and the desire to make conditions better for Indian people throughout the country. The occupiers issued a manifesto entitled "A Proclamation from the Indians of All Tribes," which called on the federal government and American people to live up to their treaty obligations with Indian peoples and to respect tribal sovereignty. A Mohawk man, Richard Oakes, played an integral role in organizing the Alcatraz occupation. Oakes also created one of the first Native American Studies programs at San Francisco State University and was a strong supporter of Indian self-determination and sovereignty. Oakes was murdered on September 20, 1972, while assisting Washington State tribes in preserving their treaty-protected fishing rights along the Columbia River.

In 1968 the American Indian Movement (AIM) was founded in Minneapolis by urban Indians such as Vernon and Clyde Bellecourt, George Mitchell, and Dennis Banks, who sought to end police brutality toward Indian people in the city, to provide educational opportunities and social services to urban Indians, to preserve ties to traditional culture on

1979

March 9 The U.S. Congress passes the Archaeological Resources Protection Act in an attempt to strengthen the protection of Indian archaeological remains.

July 16 The largest nuclear accident in the history of the United States releases more than 1,100 tons of radioactive sludge into the Rio Puerco on the Navajo reservation.

1980

June 22 Kateri Tekakwitha, a seventeenth-century Mohawk woman, is beatified by Pope John Paul II.

October 10 Congress passes the Maine Indian Land Claims Settlement Act, which provides over $80 million to compensate Native people in Maine for their land losses.

The Supreme Court upholds Lakota Sioux claims to the Black Hills and orders financial compensation of $122 million for the illegal seizure of those lands.

the reservations, and to provide legal services to Indians trying to deal with the U.S. bureaucracy and court systems. Banks, an Anishinabe Indian, played an instrumental role in leading the AIM through a series of protests against unfair treatment of Indian people by local, state, and federal officials. The AIM and Banks reached the pinnacle of public renown during the 1973 standoff between the AIM and federal law enforcement officials at Wounded Knee on the Pine Ridge reservation in South Dakota. More recently, Banks spearheaded the Sacred Run organization, which promotes awareness of Indian issues and self-confidence among Indian people. Indian activists and members of the AIM occupied the *Mayflower* replica in Plymouth, Massachusetts, on Thanksgiving Day 1970. The AIM also declared Thanksgiving a day of national mourning. A Lakota man, Russell Means, first became known to the American public through his leadership in the Mayflower occupation. Like Banks, Means went on to play an

Indian activists conducting a fish-in on the Nisqually River near Olympia, Washington, in 1966.

1982

April 17 Section 35 of Canada's Constitutional Act recognizes and affirms existing First Nations individual and treaty rights.

1983

April 11 Narragansetts in New England gain U.S. federal recognition.

October 18 Congress passes legislation granting federal recognition to the Mashantucket Pequots of Connecticut.

1985

December 5 Wilma Mankiller becomes the principal chief of the Cherokee Nation in Oklahoma.

1986

August 27 The Klamath tribe is restored to federally recognized tribal status.

After gaining federal recognition as an Indian tribe, the Mashantucket Pequot tribe in Connecticut opens a bingo gambling operation.

important leadership role in the AIM and Indian causes generally, especially in turning the AIM's attention to the Pine Ridge reservation, where he was originally from, in 1972 and 1973. Subsequently, Means has remained active in politics and in Hollywood by acting in several films, such as *Last of the Mohicans* (1992).

In 1972 the AIM sponsored the Trail of Broken Treaties national protest, which culminated in the occupation of the BIA building in Washington, D.C. The Trail of Broken Treaties brought Indians to the nation's capital from all over the country to highlight the government's record of not living up to treaty stipulations. The occupation of the BIA building was unintended but lasted for six days as more than 700 Indians ransacked files, seeking to find evidence of federal government wrongdoings. The national media latched onto the event, bringing much attention to the AIM's demands for redress of treaty violations. The Nixon administration

Members of the American Indian Movement standing guard during the occupation of Wounded Knee, 1973.

1987

March 8 The Wampanoag Tribe of Gay Head on Martha's Vineyard gains federal recognition.

August 18 Alabama-Coushatta Indians in Texas regain federal recognition.

1988

Bill Anoatubby becomes governor of the Chickasaw Nation.

October 17 Congress passes the American Indian Gaming Regulatory Act, which allows Indian tribes to negotiate with state governments to establish gambling operations.

negotiated an end to the standoff rather than risk a public relations disaster by storming the building with police or military forces. In 1973 the AIM and traditional Lakotas from the Pine Ridge reservation in South Dakota occupied a church at Wounded Knee, site of the 1890 massacre of Big Foot's people. The standoff lasted seventy-one days, and two AIM supporters were killed by forces that included U.S. marshals, the U.S. Army, the FBI, and the reservation police under the command of Pine Ridge chairman Richard Wilson. The AIM had arrived on Pine Ridge shortly after leaving Washington, D.C., and occupying the BIA building to investigate stories of Wilson's corrupt government and the racism and violence perpetrated against Indians by white communities on the borders of the reservation. The government indicted 185 AIM members for their role in the takeover at Wounded Knee, although several leaders, such as Dennis Banks, escaped before they could be arrested.

American Indian Movement leader Dennis Banks during the Trail of Broken Treaties march, 1972.

1989

Winona LaDuke, an Anishinabe woman, founds the White Earth Land Recovery Project on the White Earth Ojibwe reservation in Minnesota.

The Canadian Premier's Council on Native Affairs is created to meet First Nations and prepare recommendations to the government on a range of issues.

The Ministry of Aboriginal Affairs is formed in the Canadian government.

1990

May 29 The U.S. Supreme Court hears *Duro v. Reina*, which maintains that Indian tribes do not have jurisdiction over Indians who were not members of the particular tribe on whose lands a crime occurred.

November 6 Lumbee Indian Adolph Dial is elected to the North Carolina legislature.

July 11–September 26 The Oka Crisis takes place in Canada when Mohawk warriors engage in an armed standoff with the Quebec police and Canadian Army over land at Oka.

November 16 Congress passes the Native American Graves Protection and Repatriation Act, which requires museums and other agencies to return Indian artifacts and human remains to Indian groups.

Leonard Peltier, currently in federal prison for killing two FBI agents on the Pine Ridge reservation in 1975.

In 1975 two FBI agents died when they pursued a suspect allegedly belonging to the AIM on the Pine Ridge reservation in South Dakota. The AIM had attempted to aid members and traditional Lakotas under siege by tribal chairman Wilson's police force. In 1977 an Anishinabe man, Leonard Peltier, was convicted on dubious evidence of murdering the two FBI agents on the Pine Ridge reservation in 1975. Peltier lived on the Pine Ridge reservation at that time; a member of the AIM, he was sent to assist Pine Ridge residents under attack for opposing tribal chairman Richard Wilson. Though the case against him was circumstantial at best, and falsified at worst, a jury made up of non-Indians convicted Peltier of the murders and he is now serving two consecutive life sentences in federal prison. Attempts to reopen the case or obtain a pardon from the president of the United States have failed so far.

Self-Determination

Since 1970 the focus among Indian activists and political leaders has been on regaining as much control over their own affairs as possible. In the past four decades, there have been notable success stories within some Indian communities and in new legislation passed by the U.S. and Canadian governments. In 1968 the U.S. Congress passed the Indian Civil Rights Act, which was sponsored by North Carolina senator Sam Ervin Jr. The act emphasized civil rights for all Native Americans, but did not strengthen tribal sovereignty.

President Richard Nixon acted progressively in Indian affairs, calling for an end to termination.

1992

A report called "Misplaced Trust: The Bureau of Indian Affairs' Mismanagement of the Indian Trust Fund" is issued by the House Committee on Government Operations.

February 15 Foxwoods Casino, owned by the Mashantucket Pequots, is opened in Connecticut.

1993

November 20 The Catawbas regain federal recognition.

President Richard Nixon advanced the cause of self-determination for Indian people in a number of important ways. In his 1970 address to Congress, he called for an end to the termination program, for an indefinite continuation of the federal government's trust relationship with tribes, and for treaties to be upheld, serving as the basis for inter-governmental relations. In 1970 Nixon also oversaw the return of Blue Lake to the Taos pueblo. Blue Lake had been taken away for Kit Carson National Forest in 1906. The government offered financial compensation to Taos residents, but they refused any money while demanding the return of the lake and surrounding land. Nixon supported their position, and Blue Lake (plus 48,000 acres) once again came under Taos pueblo control. Also during Nixon's tenure as president, Congress passed the Alaska Native Claims Settlement Act to compensate Indian groups in Alaska for lands taken for use by energy companies.

A resident of the Taos pueblo in northern New Mexico, which remains vibrant.

1994

April 25 The Mohegan Tribe of Connecticut gains federal recognition.

Navajo Roberta Blackgoat is named "America's Unsung Woman" by the National Women's History Project for her decades-long work in trying to protect the environmental and cultural integrity of Black Mesa.

1995

The Mississippi Band of Choctaw Indians hires Republican lobbyist Jack Abramoff to defeat legislation that would have competed with their thriving gambling operations.

Abramoff calls the Choctaws "monkeys" and defrauds them of over $10 million, which is then funneled to Republican causes and elected officials.

August 29 The Jena Band of Choctaws in Louisiana is federally recognized.

Federal Legislation

Additional pieces of federal legislation have further strengthened Indian sovereignty since 1970. In 1978 Congress passed the Native American Religious Freedom Act, which protects Indian religious sites from being developed and gives access for Indians to religious sites now owned by others. Some impacts of this legislation have included a Wintu medicine woman being allowed to keep her healing tent in Trinity National Forest in California; customs agents no longer being allowed to search Blackfoot, Cree, and Mohawk medicine bundles as they cross the U.S.-Canadian border; the U.S. Navy granting permission to Paiutes and Shoshones to visit healing springs on the China Lake Naval Weapons Station in the Mojave Desert; and Nebraska, South Dakota, and federal prisons allowing Indian convicts to build sweat lodges for purification rites. The Religious Freedom Act was revised in 1994 to allow even more access and protection for geographic sites that are religiously important to Native Americans. In 1972 the Indian Education Act called for parental and tribal participation in federal

education programs. Money was allocated to set up community-run schools, and funding went to state and local agencies, universities, and tribes for teaching Indian history, culture, and bilingual courses. This act marked the first time since the founding of the United States that Indians were given control over their own education in any significant way. The Indian Self-Determination and Education Assistance Act of 1975 further restored tribal control over education and sovereignty. In 1978 Congress passed the American Indian Child Welfare Act, which dramatically lessened the practice of taking Indian children away from their families for adoption by non-Indians.

In 1979 Congress passed the Archaeological Resources Protection Act in an attempt to strengthen the protection of Indian archaeological remains, such as the estimated 4,000 Anasazi cliff houses destroyed in the strip mining of the coal of Black Mesa on Hopi and Navajo lands in Arizona. In 1980 Congress passed the Maine Indian Land Claims

....

Petroglyphs located on Department of Defense lands, Naval Weapons Station, China Lake, California.

1996

An audit of tribal trust funds maintained by the Bureau of Indian Affairs on behalf of Indian people is found to be missing $2.4 billion.

June 10 Elouise Cobell files a lawsuit against the U.S. Department of the Interior, seeking missing Indian trust fund monies.

A judge rules in favor of the Navajos who sued the Peabody Coal Company's owners for not abiding by permit requirements, and for polluting the air, land, and water on the reservation.

Winona LaDuke runs for vice president of the United States on the Green Party ticket.

Settlement Act, which provided over $80 million to compensate Native people in Maine for their land losses and to enable them to reacquire some land. In the same year, the U.S. Supreme Court upheld Lakota Sioux claims to the Black Hills and ordered financial compensation of $122 million for the illegal seizure of those lands. The Lakotas refused the money on the grounds that they wanted the land and never intended to sell the Black Hills. In 1982 Canada's Constitutional Act, Section 35, recognized and affirmed existing First Nations individual and treaty rights. In 1988 Congress passed the American Indian Gaming Regulatory Act, which allowed federally recognized Indian tribes to negotiate with state governments to establish gambling operations. In 1990 Congress passed the Native American Graves Protection and Repatriation Act, which requires museums and other agencies that receive federal funding to return Indian artifacts and human remains when requested to do so.

Anasazi Indian ruins, now part of the Navajo National Monument.

1997

Ms. Magazine names Winona LaDuke "Woman of the Year."

Creek poet and musician Joy Harjo wins the Lila Wallace Reader's Digest Fund Writer's Award.

1999

February 22 Department of the Interior Secretary Bruce Babbitt, head of the Bureau of Indian Affairs Kevin Gover, and Treasury Secretary Robert Rubin are found in contempt of court in the scandal over missing Indian trust fund monies.

2000

Around 4.1 million Americans claim on the Census to be wholly or partly Native American.

Winona LaDuke again runs for vice president of the United States on the Green Party ticket.

September 8 Kevin Gover issues a formal apology to American Indians for its legacy of "racism and inhumanity."

Despite these positive developments in intergovernmental relations between Indian groups and the U.S. and Canadian governments, numerous hardships exist for Indian people. They still combat stereotypes, such as the use of Indians for sports mascots like the Washington Redskins football team or the widely held belief that all Indians today are wealthy from gambling revenues. Issues of sovereignty, control over land, cultural survival, and identity remain highly sensitive and contested. As has always been the case, especially after Europeans and others arrived in the Americas over 500 years ago, Indians find themselves living in a world of constant change, and it requires due diligence to adapt and survive.

Cathedral Spires located on land held sacred and claimed by the Lakota Sioux in the Black Elk Wilderness, Black Hills, South Dakota.

2002

September 17 Department of the Interior Secretary Gale Norton is held in contempt of court for failing to provide documentation relating to the Indian trust fund and the missing billions.

2004

September 21 The National Museum of the American Indian is opened on the Mall in Washington, D.C.

2006

January 3 Jack Abramoff pleads guilty to federal charges of conspiracy, fraud, and tax evasion for his lobbying actions on behalf of Indian tribes.

Index